Growing Together

GROWING TOGETHER

A Manual for Councils of Churches

NATIONAL COUNCIL of the CHURCHES of CHRIST in the U.S.A.

Library of Congress No. 55-11909

Copyright 1955
Printed in the U.S.A.
NATIONAL COUNCIL OF CHURCHES

CONTENTS· ·

5

7

FOREWORD ·

GROWING TOGETHER, a Manual for Councils of Churches, has been designed primarily to assist the hundreds of persons serving as officers or staff members in councils of churches. The Central Department of Field Administration of the National Council of Churches initiated the preparation of this Manual at the meeting of its Board of Managers in November, 1953. A special committee was appointed by the Board consisting of Willis R. Ford, chairman, John B. Ketcham, J. Quinter Miller, Minor C. Miller, William D. Powell, Mrs. William Sale Terrell and Mrs. Fred H. White. This committee was authorized to proceed with the project.

The committee, which has prepared the Manual, hopes that it will be used by councils of churches that are served by either employed or voluntary leadership, by denominational personnel, by the staff members of national interdenominational agencies, and student and faculty members of seminaries, colleges, and universities.

The Manual provides answers to such questions as, "What is a council of churches?" "How is it constituted?" "What is its organizational structure?" "What is the character of its program?" and many other important questions.

The authors, whose names appear at the beginning of each chapter, have volunteered their services. The substance of the material presented in each chapter is the responsibility of the author.

The Project Committee has made minor editorial revisions of the manuscript in order to secure greater coherence and to eliminate certain obvious duplications. The editorial work of H. Robinson Shipherd helped immensely in the final preparation of the manuscript for publication. The manuscript was read by all members of the committee, and by members of the special committee appointed by Glenn W. Moore, chairman of the General Committee on Program and Field Operations of the National Council of Churches, which included Leila W. Anderson, Roswell P. Barnes, C. Franklin Koch, and Mrs. Arthur Sherman.

The views expressed in this publication are those of the authors and are not to be construed as declarations of official attitudes or policies of the National Council of Churches or any of its units.

Willis R. Ford, *chairman*
J. Quinter Miller, *staff executive*

Chapter 1

HISTORY

· ·

R. W. Sanderson

Where and when did this co-operation of churches across denominational lines begin?

Not at any one time or place; it is a long, complicated story, as yet written only in fragments. We have space here to spell out only a few of its main outlines. In it are several strands, like the wires, with their different colored insulations, woven into a single electrical unit.

Co-operative Christianity in America had its beginning in the area of Christian education. The earliest convention of Sunday school workers was held under the auspices of the American Sunday School Union in 1824. The first national Sunday school convention was held in Philadelphia in 1832; the second and third national conventions were held in the same city in 1833 and 1859; the fourth national convention met at Newark, New Jersey, in 1869. Thus it was that laymen of many denominations learned to work together and to like it before the beginning of the last quarter of the nineteenth century.

In 1872, in Indianapolis, Indiana, the first international Sunday school convention approved basic principles and plans for a system of Sunday school lessons for the churches of America. When or where has there ever occurred a more significant event in the total field of co-operative Christianity?

In 1910 the official representatives of several denominational agencies for Sunday school work united to form the Sunday School Council of evangelical denominations. For more than a decade this new organization paralleled the older and well established International Sunday School Association. In 1922, in Kansas City, these two streams of Sunday school effort united to form the International Council of Religious Education. In 1950, in Cleveland, Ohio, the International Council of Religious Education was merged with other agencies to form the National Council of Churches.

The Field Is the World

The foreign missionary movement began, as far as America is concerned, under a haystack in western Massachusetts a century and a half ago. Shortly it was denominationalized; but the great foreign boards soon discovered, even before their home-base churches did, that it was foolish and wrong for denominations to compete with one another unfairly in the vast task of world

11

evangelization. So they gave each other the chance to begin and continue noncompetitively, and to present far from home a united front. When disaster struck—as it repeatedly did—and new beginnings were necessary, the boards and their missionaries faced their tasks together. For example, in 1901, after the Boxer uprising, one mission in China considered "Comity, Co-operation, and Delimitation of Boundaries."

By 1910 the time was ripe for a great missionary conference in Edinburgh, out of which flowed mighty tides of church co-operation. One of these, called "Life and Work," culminated in Stockholm in 1925 and in Oxford in 1937. The other, called "Faith and Order," led to Lausanne in 1927, and Edinburgh in 1937. In 1910 in Edinburgh the churches in "mission" lands were represented by about 30 people out of 1,300. At Jerusalem in 1928 the term, "younger churches," often used not too accurately, came into general use. By 1938 in Madras, where nearly half the delegates came as representatives of the younger churches, and again at Willingen in 1952, the great churches of the West found themselves conferring with churches that were the logical outcome of the missionary enterprise, ancient and modern.

In 1937, on the eve of Oxford and Edinburgh, members of both the "Life and Work" and the "Faith and Order" groups met in London. In 1938, at Utrecht, a provisional constitution was adopted for the World Council of Churches, to be long "in process of formation." Then came World War II. It was not until 1948, in Amsterdam, that the World Council was fully organized. By that time the ecclesiastical climate of the world had markedly changed; the world was proving "too much for a divided Church." In Evanston, in 1954, the Second Assembly of the World Council of Churches confirmed anew the intention of its 163 member communions not only "to stay together" but "to grow together." The church had thus achieved new centrality in the thinking of all.

Of Such Is the Kingdom of Heaven

A major factor in the life of the church in the nineteenth century has been the world-wide organization of Sunday schools: the child was once more being brought into the center. At first the secular and lay-led Sunday schools became the chief feeders of the churches. Denominations organized Sunday school and youth departments, later inclusive of all types of Christian education. In America the states, cities, counties, even townships, provided a vast network of conventions. In every land the work with childhood and youth, as well as various forms of adult education, became an important part of church life. Accordingly there is a third organization, the World Council of Christian Education and Sunday School Association, also co-operative with but separate from the World Council of Churches.

The United States Blazes a New Trail

Separate churches that want to do things together have found out how to organize to get these various functions performed. So the Foreign Missions

12

Conference was organized in 1893; and the Federal Council of Churches, the Home Missions Council, and the Missionary Education Movement were organized in 1908. As stated earlier, in 1922 in Kansas City the International Council of Religious Education was organized—"international" because it served Canada as well as the United States. The basis of representation was dual—by denominations, but also by state councils.

Meanwhile state councils of churches and home missions and local councils or federations had sprung up. The earliest state organization was the International Commission of Maine, dating from 1891. Its specific task was to avoid hopeless denominational rivalry in small fields. In 1895 the Federation of Churches and Christian Workers in New York city was organized "to bring the intelligence and love of our churches to bear upon the material, social, economic, civic, and spiritual interests of the family life of our city, through interdenominational conference and co-operation to meet its every religious and moral need." This ambitious program it attacked along significant but highly specialized lines, which have affected the gathering of census data in every metropolitan center.

Apostles of Christian unity had not been lacking, neither had co-operative agencies. As early as 1864 Samuel S. Schmucker had presented a historic "Overture for Christian Union." In 1893 Philip Schaff spoke on "The Reunion of Christendom." These were powerful and persuasive voices, but they did not galvanize the churches into action. Similarly the Evangelical Alliance, which in the early nineteen hundred's preceded the organization of the Federal Council, had had comparatively small effect on actual church life in parishes, communions, and communities. The student Christian movement enlisted and trained many persons who have contributed leadership to various phases of the ecumenical movement. The Y.M.C.A. and the Y.W.C.A. also trained many leaders, and brought Christian people together throughout the world.

It was chiefly the interest in Christianizing the social order that finally brought about the organization of the National Federation of Churches and Christian Workers in 1900. These were the days of small and difficult beginnings, but they led to a conference in New York in 1905, which three years later in Philadelphia resulted in the organization of the Federal Council of Churches, an organization primarily related to "Life and Work." It began with district offices, and its constitution provided for local "branches"; but from the outset local and state councils were autonomous, and the federal controls were denominational.

Meanwhile the Home Missions Council had also been organized in 1908, and in a number of states there were similar bodies, where the situation was not yet ripe for councils of churches. "Master lists" sought to avoid wasteful competition in the use of church extension funds.

Other agencies, to perform other functions, had likewise sprung up. One was the Missionary Education Movement (Friendship Press), another the United Stewardship Council, a third the United Council of Church Women.

13

"It is a far cry from the 'Female Society for Missionary Purposes' organized by the Congregational and Baptist women of Boston in 1800 to the General Department of United Church Women. In those early days women thought in terms of pennies rather than dollars, and they had a long row to hoe before they won the right to 'speak in meeting' or to vote. But their thoughts and prayers circled the globe, and they gave their egg money and their sons and daughters to the mission fields. As their interests grew their numbers grew, until all over the country there were local interdenominational organizations of church women meeting together for worship, study, and action. Their representatives came together in Boston in 1929, and formed the National Council of Federated Church Women. They set up a joint committee to work with the national denominational women's boards through the Council of Women for Home Missions and the Federation of Women's Boards of Foreign Missions. In 1941 the three bodies came together in one organization, and thus joined the two national mission groups with the grass-roots local council movement across the country. Out of this union was born the United Council of Church Women."*

Accordingly there was now a wealth of national groups that together provided channels of church co-operation. Within a few decades it became evident that the varied functions thus organized had one common origin—the church itself. Particularly from "the field," which was perplexed and sometimes irritated by the complexity of the overhead ecumenical apparatus, pressures cumulatively mounted to unite all these national phases of church co-operation into one comprehensive body. This was enthusiastically accomplished, after long and careful planning, in Cleveland, in 1950. Once consummated, the National Council of the Churches of Christ in the U.S.A. drew to itself additional functional agencies.

Long before Cleveland, however, seven of the national interdenominational bodies had united their outreach in an Inter-Council Field Department for developing co-operative relationships with states and communities and in some respects with communions.

At the world level three great agencies, i.e., the World Council of Churches, the International Missionary Council, and the World Council of Christian Education, along with other significant organizations, all co-operate. At the local level foreign missions is still a cause largely promoted denominationally rather than co-operatively. At the national level all our ecumenical eggs are in one basket. Short of organic union, which many do not desire, the National Council of Churches represents functional integration that in terms of voluntary co-operation is truly massive in its proportions.

The few thousands of dollars assembled with difficulty at the turn of the century have now become a budget of more than ten million dollars. Instead of the unofficial co-operation of individuals and churches, which often ignored the established ecclesiastical lines, practical ecumenicity has at last become

---

* From the *Biennial Report 1954*, National Council of the Churches of Christ in the U.S.A.

truly the co-operation of the communions themselves, with recognition of the experience gained at local, state, and national levels.

Meanwhile, as the ecclesiastical climate continued to change in the world and in the nation, state and local councils of churches multiplied tremendously. We turn now to a quick summary of how this took place.

State and Local Councils

As has been shown, there were state and local councils long before the churches, as such, began to get together on the national and world levels; but until the denominations themselves began to co-operate, co-operation at the state and local levels was highly precarious. Church federations—as they were usually called—were born, struggled along, died, or had to be completely and repeatedly reorganized. The idea stayed alive, but organizational vigor was meager for several decades.

In 1912 a survey showed a long list of state, city, and county federations of churches, completely or partly organized; but in 1915 there were only twelve salaried executives of federations of churches, and some of those were on part time. At that time the organized Sunday school movement was far more impressive. "In 1917, for example, there were 63 state and provincial Sunday school associations; 2,592 county Sunday school associations; approximately 10,000 township Sunday school associations; and many flourishing city associations. These associations employed 300 paid workers on full time, and commanded the services of 267,307 other workers without remuneration."[*]

But the logic of events was at work. The Men and Religion Forward Movement sowed the seeds of church co-operation, and developed leadership, national and local. In October 1917 the Congress on Purpose and Methods of Interchurch Federations, held in Pittsburgh, Pennsylvania, resulted in a significant *Manual of Interchurch Work*. Then World War I intervened. In June 1920 the Church and Community Conference, held in Cleveland, resulted in a new volume, *Community Programs for Co-operating Churches*. In those days when a score or two dozen church federation secretaries got together in annual conference it was a big meeting. There were far more religious education council secretaries at their meetings.

The Interchurch World Movement came and went, leaving a deposit of facts that would prove useful in less impatient co-operation. Depression days slowed down all co-operative processes, yet at the same time re-enforced the sense of the necessity of co-operation and the folly of divided interdenominational forces.

By 1922 the central importance of state councils of churches was glimpsed. That year the Conference of Allied Church Agencies was held in Washington, D. C. As yet, however, state bodies had not proved very durable. In 1924 three—Connecticut, Massachusetts, and Ohio—had full-time executives; two—California and Pennsylvania—had part-time leadership. State councils of re-

---

[*] Walter Scott Athearn, *Religious Education and American Democracy*, Boston, Pilgrim Press, 1917, p. 195.

ligious education were as yet far more significant, in terms of budget and personnel.

Then integration gathered momentum—first at the local level slowly, and still more slowly at the state level; first in terms of professional fellowship, then in organizational expression; finally at the national level. Time was when ECOA (Employed Council Officers' Association) commanded the loyalty of the community leaders in line with the Sunday school tradition. Similarly, AES (Association of Executive Secretaries of church federations, state and local), commanded the loyalty of leaders in line with the church tradition. Now, whatever the organizational relationships, the ecumenical staff in America operates, in spite of its huge numbers, with an increasing sense of unity. When it assembles in annual conference it presents a highly trained body of hundreds of paid servants of the church, all thinking interdenominationally.

Recent Accelerated Increase

This tremendous expansion of state and local church co-operation did not come suddenly or early. As late as 1928 Charles S. Macfarland wrote, after "Twenty Years of Church Federation" at the national level: "We have been far from realizing the earliest hope in the extension of the co-operative movement in cities, states, and towns, but there has been developed at least a body of experience in a few states and some towns which is adequate so far as experimentation and demonstration was concerned."* Dr. Macfarland looked forward to "renewed progress." The facts have amply justified that hope.

There are various measures of this increase of strength.

First, there is the sheer number of councils. In 1955 state councils with paid secretaries numbered forty; and only seven states lacked a state-wide interdenominational organization of churches. Every state had a council of church women. In all, there were 260 state and local (city or county) units with paid staffs. In addition there were 699 councils operating with voluntary leadership. Councils of church women numbered 2,056; and there was a record of 2,045 ministerial associations, many of which are expanding into councils of churches.

Second, the work of the councils is more varied. Consider the table of contents of this Manual; or thumb through the first half of the list of paid council staffs in the *Yearbook of American Churches*. Besides general executives and their chief associates or assistants one finds employed staffs in such areas of work as: audio-visual education, agricultural migrant work, boys' court, chaplaincies (institutional and industrial), children's work, Christian education, church music, church world service, and Christian rural overseas program, communications, evangelism, race and intercultural relations, radio and television, research and planning, rural field work, social welfare, case worker and group worker and special projects, United Church Men, United Church Women, vacation church schools, weekday teachers and supervisors, and

---

* Macfarland, Charles S., *Twenty Years of Church Federation*, New York, Federal Council of Churches, 1929, page 34.

youth work. Such portfolios group themselves in varied patterns, and many of them subdivide naturally into differing specialties.

Third, local and state budgets have expanded, partly because the dollar buys less now, but far more largely because the volume of work has so greatly increased. Accordingly in 1953 it was found that the total income of city and county councils with paid leadership amounted to over four million dollars; state councils reported an additional two million dollars; councils without paid leadership nearly one million more—making a grand total, below the national level and in addition to it, of more than seven million.

Fourth—and a still better index of progress—is the sense of proprietorship felt by thousands of local churches, which regard these hundreds of councils as *their* co-operative associations. Theological seminaries in increasing numbers offer courses about the co-operative church task. Vocationally the challenge of entering ecumenical service is greatly increased; and there are real beginnings of nationwide personnel policy as to enlistment, in-service training, retirement, etc. Both the denominations and the general public now regard interdenominational work as an essential part of the Christian task. One may hazard the guess that in the increasingly ecumenical future the local and state councils will discover anew both the mission and the unity of the church, the depth of meaning in the Gospel, and the exceeding richness of God's grace.

Half a century ago the churches saw a few things they could do together better than they could do them separately. There are some functions that can be performed only in the local church, some by the churches denominationally, others by the churches co-operatively. The burden of proof has begun to shift to the other foot. The list of tasks done denominationally grows shorter; the number of those that are better done co-operatively grows ever longer. The church with a mission is discovering the oneness of its task. The evangel that goes out to the ends of the earth is increasingly recognized as a summons also to the churches in Mediopolis and Megalopolis, in every commonwealth and nation, to recognize their essential oneness.

Chapter 2

WHAT IS A COUNCIL OF CHURCHES?
. . . .

Wilbur C. Parry

A council of churches is an officially approved and constituted agency of a group of churches and/or communions that desire to forward certain phases of their work in co-operation with one another.

A council of churches is not *a* church. It does not presume to have a creed, or to determine right or wrong theology, or to administer the sacraments. Ideas and practices on these matters vary so greatly that no council of churches could possibly speak for all of its member churches or communions.

A council of churches is a part of *the* church, in that it is established to help forward and demonstrate the will of God as revealed by Jesus Christ. Its purposes and practices are as thoroughly Christian as those of its member communions, whose leaders recognize that it is a truly essential part of *the* Church of Christ.

At all levels, a council of churches should have the official authorization of its member churches. In a local community the council should be constituted by the official action of its member congregations. A state council of churches should be constituted by the official action of the recognized state organizations of the member communions, such as synods, conventions, conferences, or dioceses. The National and World Councils of Churches have been constituted by the official action of the member communions. In all cases, the constituting group for a council of churches must be those representatives who have been appointed and authorized by their respective churches.

After a council of churches has been duly organized by this authorization of its member churches and/or communions, it may then include in its boards and committees members at large or representatives of other approved organizations. Such representatives, if given the power to vote, should be members in good standing of one of the member communions, or of a communion approved by the representatives of the member communions. It should always be clear that a council of churches is representative of the churches, and is not just another religious or community organization. Though this limits its freedom, it adds to its strength. On this basis, a council of churches may perhaps not speak as often; but when it does speak, it speaks as the official representative of a sizable group of Christian men, women, and young people.

It should always be recognized that a council of churches in no way legally

18

or technically destroys the autonomy of its member churches. They may decide to co-operate on one project and not to co-operate on another. But those churches that constitute a council of churches have by their act signified their intention to do those things together that they believe can be done together as well or better than separately. Both of these facts may not always be recognized by council officers and executives or leaders of the member churches; but it is essential that they be clearly recognized if a council of churches is to be established effectively.

Besides direct representation from the communions that constitute the council of churches it may be advantageous to include representation from councils of churches that serve more localized areas. For example, a state council of churches might well have representation in its central governing and planning group from city or county councils, as the National Council now has representatives from the co-operative work of the churches on the state and local levels. If such representation from the local councils is a part of the organizational pattern for area state and national councils, it should be understood that the local council agrees with the purposes of the larger council, and that both are representative of the communions in their areas.

Chapter 3

PHILOSOPHY

. . . .

J. Quinter Miller

Councils of churches are the groundwork of Christian co-operation. They are a timely response to the desire of many Christians to work together. The growing number of these councils and the expansion of their program of activity throughout the United States is the significant fact of present-day religious history. Why are councils of churches created, and how do they happen to be what they are? This guidebook aims to provide some answers to these questions.

In this chapter will be presented a comprehensive view of the nature of the experience that churches have as they work with each other in councils of churches. There is a systematic body of general conceptions or principles now operative within the council-of-churches movement, and a presentation of them may help to furnish a philosophical foundation for its further growth and development.

Wherever churches wish to be together in the "spirit of oneness" they must manifest that spirit of oneness in the community. In order to move a building, we have to begin by moving the base of the structure; and since the building rests on that base, it will move as the base is moved. This, in a sense, is symbolic of the way in which churches must move and act together. The nature of their co-operative service demands that they have an organization that is philosophically sound, and proved by experience to be trustworthy. This is why the foundation must be sound.

There are certain principles within a council-of-churches operation that provide a philosophical foundation that encourages steady growth and development. These principles have been tested and proved in the experience of many communities, small and large, and are therefore widely recognized today as basic ideas that tend to shape the course of Christian co-operation throughout the ecumenical movement. There are, of course, certain councils of churches whose experience does not exemplify all the principles here outlined; the embryonic character of some councils and the degree of their functional growth account for their many individual differences. But when we try to think truly about the meaning of the co-operative work of the churches as a whole, certain principles become clearly apparent. These we shall now consider.

20

The Representative Principle

When the governing body of a council of churches is composed of the representatives that have been designated by congregations or communions, it is *representatively* constituted. When separate Christian congregations and communions wish to work with other Christian congregations and communions, they need a representatively constituted joint agency. The representatives chosen should consist of laymen, laywomen, youth, and ministers who are competent both denominationally and departmentally to think, plan, and act with authority to regulate the council of churches proceedings in accordance with its constitution and bylaws in behalf of the appointing bodies (congregations locally, communions in states). The decisions made and the activities conducted thus become a co-operative expression of responsibly authorized Christian endeavor. By means of this principle of representation, otherwise separate and divided congregations and communions can perform common tasks; the work done together is the achievement of the co-operating congregations and communions. A council of churches so constituted is the representative agent of its member congregations.

The Evangelical Principle

Evangelical churches adhere to that interpretation of Christianity that emphasizes man's weakness to sin, Christ's saving power, and the need of a new birth and redemption through faith. The doctrinal phrase: "Jesus Christ as Divine Lord and Savior," is generally incorporated in the preamble to the constitution of councils of churches. By means of such a statement in the preamble, the member churches seek clearly to establish the fact that they are partners in a Christian fellowship that is striving to witness to its faith in a Godlike Christ and a Christlike God. They also wish to show that it is their purpose to witness to their evangelical faith by means of the life and work, of the councils of churches in which they share control. The full adherence to this evangelical principle requires that only those representatives may vote in the governing body of the council who have been appointed or approved by their respective evangelical congregations and communions. To be sure, provision is generally made for an affiliate relationship, short of voting membership, for those nonevangelical bodies who may wish to participate in certain activities and services. Such affiliated bodies do not appoint voting representatives to the governing body of the council of churches.

The Principle of Affiliation

There are a number of organizations that have a Christian purpose but that do not qualify as evangelical churches and hence are ineligible for membership in a council of churches; and these Christian organizations frequently desire to participate in the activities that member churches undertake together through their council. Each local or state council of churches shall determine the conditions under which such moral and religious agencies as desire to co-operate may do so. The principle of affiliation suggests that an advisory, consultative, or co-operative relationship, short of full membership, may be established. Affiliated organizations of moral and spiritual character may thereby be accorded the right to participate in conferences and other program activities, though such affiliation does not carry with it voting privileges in the governing body of the council.

The Principle of Local Autonomy

American co-operative Christianity consists of many autonomous units: neighborhood, city, county, trade area, state, and national councils. Each council of churches is locally autonomous; that is, the polity of its government is congregational: there is no authority or control exercised by one council over another. Each is free to determine its own type of organization, and to outline and carry out its own program, under the supervision of its member congregations or communions. Structurally, councils of churches are self-governing bodies. This principle of local autonomy recognizes the validity of the judgment of its constituent member bodies. Adherence to this principle implies the freedom to choose, to differ, or to modify present practices in order to become a part of a larger voluntary fellowship. There are, however, ties of fellowship among councils of churches that are functional, experiential, and spiritual. The sense of fellowship that results from such voluntary association signifies a "togetherness of purpose" within the whole ecumenical family, even when a conclusion reached by a given council may vary from current ecumenical practice. This principle of autonomy enhances the local spirit of ecumenicity.

The Principle of Inclusiveness

Protestant-Orthodox Christianity achieves a greater functional solidarity and effectiveness when it can work harmoniously together in one inclusive organization. The program of co-operative work in evangelism, Christian education, Christian social relations, Christian missions, public relations, pastoral services, corporate worship, and the program projects of the general departments of young people, laymen, laywomen, and clergymen comprises the responsibly authorized Christian ministry of the co-operating churches. One all-inclusive council of churches, which will comprise all these services, is the ideal of this principle of inclusiveness. In areas where there are two or more co-operative agencies, the practice of living together in fellowship and working together on common activities has proved a most fruitful first step toward fuller co-operation. Constitutional provisions, though necessary, do not penetrate to the root of the problem. Sharing equitably in the administration of common activities to attain common ends and then working together for these ends are the best approaches for securing complete program and organizational integration.

The Functional Principle

The discovery of the major problems of religious living, the search for solutions to these problems, and the development of organizational patterns through which these discoveries may be made and worked out, characterize the functional basis of community organization. When this principle is followed, "function" is the determiner of "structure." The needs for action and service that churches experience in their ministry in their communities, become the determining factors in their organizational growth and development. Adherence to this principle makes for creativeness; and there is always a down-to-earth quality in the programs that are developed on this principle. The work undertaken has a life-giving vitality about it, because the needs that such activity seeks to meet are recognized as actual and real. "Functions should determine structure, and *not* structure, function."

The Principle of Committee Integration

The organization of the co-operative work of the churches along such functional lines generally includes departments and committees. The larger councils may also provide for divisions and commissions. The administration of the work of such units is enhanced when those that have natural functional relationships are grouped as a department or a division. This practice helps to integrate the programs of related units. This grouping of similar functions is also useful for staff specialization and supervision.

There is no single pattern in current practice; likewise, the words, "department" and "commission," are often used interchangeably. The example that follows is prompted by the current use within the National Council of the words "division," "department," and "committee."

1. *Program Division*
   a. Christian Education
      Committees on—The Religious Education of Children
      The Religious Education of Youth
      The Religious Education of Adults
      Leadership Training
      Christian Family Life
      Audio-Visual Education
      Vacation Church Schools
      Weekday Church Schools
   b. Christian Life and Work
      Committees on—Christian Social Relations:
      Church and Economic Life
      Legislative Action
      Liquor Control
      Racial and Cultural Relations
      International Affairs
      Evangelism and Worship
      Ministry in Institutions
      Pastoral Services
      Social Welfare
      Stewardship and Benevolence

23

c. Christian Missions and Services
   Committees on—Friendly Relations among Foreign Students
                      Ministry to Migrants
                      Missionary Education
                      Survey and Church Planning
                      Town and Country Church (in State Councils)
                      Urban Church (in State Councils)
                      Church World Service

2. General Departments
   a. Ministerial Fellowship
   b. United Church Men
   c. United Church Women
   d. Youth Fellowship

3. Central Departments
   a. Public Relations
   b. Business and Finance
   c. Field Administration (in State Councils)
   d. Radio and Television

Since there is no uniformity of practice, further experience in applying this principle of committee integration is needed before final conclusions can be reached. The outline suggested by the above example is being adopted in a number of states and cities. Should this prove generally acceptable, the chief gain will be similar function groupings, with readier communication, among national, state, city, and local councils.

The Principle of Committee Membership

The word, "committee," means a person or persons to whom some trust or charge is committed. Councils of churches have committees of many types. The groupings of committees with similar functions into departments and divisions is a common administrative practice.

What is the principle that should be followed by a council of churches in selecting persons to serve on its various committees, departments, and divisions? It is this: Select competent people from the constituent churches or communions to whom the member churches and the units have entrusted similar functions or responsibilities. When this principle is applied, the resulting committee becomes a united body through which the work of the member churches and the general departments may be co-operatively planned and executed; and adherence to this principle extends the work of local churches outward into the community.

At the same time this procedure connects the work of a committee of a council of churches with the program committees and boards of the member churches and communions from which its committee membership is drawn. The operation of this principle makes for program co-ordination.

24

The Principle of Co-operative Responsibility

The co-operative work of the churches belongs to them. It is their responsibility. It is not extrachurch, nor is it suprachurch. It is the mutual responsibility of the partnership that the member congregations or communions have created. They are therefore jointly responsible for those phases of its work that by their representative participation they have mutually authorized. The programs of the council, so formulated, constitute an integral part of the member churches' own programs and responsibilities, and deserve the full support of each constituent member. This principle of shared responsibility through voluntary co-operation is a fundamental principle of all really ecumenical endeavor.

The Principle of Financial Integrity

The financial integrity of the member congregations and communions of a council of churches is measured partly by the degree to which they carry their share of the cost of their co-operative work. Since a council is the joint possession of its member bodies and a projection of their ministry, they share mutually in its cost. The proportion of its cost can be computed as follows:

1. Divide the budget of the council of churches by the sum of the current expense and benevolence income of the member bodies.
2. Multiply the current expense and benevolence budget of the member congregation or communion by the percentage resulting from Step 1.

The resulting sum equals the actual share that each partner church or communion should contribute in financing the co-operative work it conducts through its council of churches. The financial stability and integrity of the churches' co-operative work depends, in the long run, on the degree in which this principle of financial integrity is established and followed.

The Principle of Efficient Business Management

The business and financial affairs of councils of churches should be efficiently managed. The member churches and the general departments are filled with men and women who have the technical know-how of business efficiency. These skills can contribute significantly to the quality of the service that the churches give together, and should be sought as an important avenue of Christian vocation. Among the marks of efficient business management we know that financial records are audited by a Certified Public Accountant. Credit is kept good by the prompt payment of all bills; personnel practices provide for job analysis, salary scale, promotion, vacation, health insurance, and pension and retirement regulations. Attention should likewise be given to the improvement of the equipment and facilities needed in the work of councils of churches.

The Principle of Lay Participation

The influence, vision, and understanding of Christian laymen and laywomen are a principal asset of protestantism; and of course this source of strength is needed in all effective Christian co-operation. The deliberative and program-building activities of councils of churches are strengthened by the degree in which laymen and laywomen, young people, and clergymen share together their separate insights and experiences to develop the co-operative work of the churches. Business and professional men and women, homemakers, farmers, employees and employers, students, teachers, and church officials can contribute valuable experience and accept individual responsibility for many program and administrative activities. Therefore lay participation is sought in each functional activity, in addition to the special fellowship groupings and activities that general departments may provide. *A strong council of churches is representative of the total life of its member congregations and communions,* which means the participation of laymen, laywomen, young people, and clergymen in all program operations.

The Principle of the Prophetic

A council of churches needs to see its task in the light of what the churches ought to be doing together: How shall the co-operating churches lift up Christ in order that all men may be drawn unto him? This principle of the prophetic is a co-operative endeavor to put ourselves and our churches under the judgment of Christ, responsive to his calling, his prompting, and his sending. As churches seek co-operatively to do this, they realize that the manifestation of their unity with Christ in the life of the community cannot be fully achieved until "each part is working properly"—only then is the body of Christ truly upbuilded in love. A council of churches that is prophetic must be outreaching in its search for new ways to further the cause of Christ. A council is not measuring up to its full opportunity until it speaks to the needs of this age with a prophetic voice!

The Principle of Unity in Diversity

Christian co-operation of churches, and of individuals in the churches, is the prevailing expression of Christian unity in America. This unity is grounded in a great central core of Christian conviction held in common by the co-operating denominations that reveals an identifiable common mind. Although American communions have a varied heritage of Christian faith and practice, there has emerged a common spirit of sharing that is a model of the democratic ideal and temper of American life. This common spirit has enabled the churches to unite in their effort to create a Christian land governed by Christian principles. Some churches may not always be ready to support all the program activities that councils of churches undertake, because of the diversity of their histories and insights; this fact we must acknowledge and accept. But regardless of such diversity, a common Christian outlook, which is far more important than denominational divisions, makes for wide ranges of co-operative Christian unity.

The Principle of Service as Authority

A council of churches is a council composed of churches. Through it the member churches take counsel together about their work. As a council, it has no *authority* over its member churches; the moral impact of its actions and the value of its program of activities constitute its authority. In this sense its only authority is derivative, resulting from the intrinsic value of the common judgments expressed and the good resulting from the service given. A scriptural basis for this principle is found in the words of Jesus, where he said, "Whoever would be great among you must be your servant" (Mark 10:43).

Conclusion

These foregoing principles specify the basic groundwork for Christian co-operation as developed today by councils of churches. They are not only a portrait of what now is—they are that because they have been largely deduced from day-to-day experience. But they are also a guide to the future growth and the improvement of council structure. In Chapter 5 these principles will be applied to sample constitutions for councils of churches.

The philosophy herein presented sees the churches' co-operative work as integral to the life and witness of the member congregations, and not something separate and apart from them. No man or group can make the churches one. "But Christ has made us his own, and he is not divided."* When we come closer to him we find one another.

---

* *The First Assembly of the World Council of Churches*, New York, Harper and Brothers, 1948, page 9.

Chapter 4

STEPS IN ORGANIZATION
· ·

John B. Ketcham

The Need for a Council

This chapter assumes that there are at least a few churches in your community that wish to affirm their oneness in Jesus Christ and their desire to express their "togetherness" by carrying on some of their responsibilities co-operatively with other churches. Perhaps they have done so informally for a long time, but now want an organization that will more adequately express their common concerns. Your situation may involve only a few churches, or many. Perhaps your population totals only a few thousand persons; or perhaps it numbers ten thousand or many more. Whatever your situation, the broad principles here suggested will be found, with proper modification of detail, to apply in general to all local councils.

Prepare the Ground Carefully

The possibilities of a council of churches for the community and the kingdom are so great that it is important to interest enough people in advance of any organization meeting, however informal, to assure positive action. Until this is possible, do not force the issue. "Shall we or shall we not?" is a question that might better be postponed until it more or less becomes "When do we begin? How do we start?"

Informal Personal Discussion

Read carefully this entire book, particularly Chapters 2 and 3, to make sure that you have the basic idea of what a council is, what it does, how it can be organized, how it may be financed. Study carefully the special needs of your community. Get several key persons to read this book and begin thinking about these questions. Then spend some time discussing the whole matter informally with other key individuals whose influence is likely to be essential to the council's success. These key persons should include outstanding laymen, laywomen, and the pastors of the several churches. Talk with them separately. Get them to read this book. Bring two or three together to discuss various aspects of the problem. Allow a long enough interval to elapse to be sure the first enthusiasm is enduring. "Strike while the iron is hot" is a good maxim, but there needs to be a forge of intelligent support in which the iron can be kept hot. This preliminary stage of informal discussion can save time in the end.

Informal Discussion with Existing Co-operating Groups

In your community there may be a council of church women, a youth council, or a ministerial association. Bring together the presidents of these organizations and informally discuss the value to them of co-operation among the churches, the basic principles in Chapter 3, and the relation of their organizations to a council of churches. The local council of church women or the local ministerial association, or both groups working together and acting through a carefully chosen committee, may properly take the lead during this informal discussion period. Whatever the group, it should take time to study carefully the foundation principles, and to seek more answers to the questions in the next sections.

Hold an Informal Conference

When sufficient interest seems to warrant it, a meeting of representative pastors, lay leaders, both men and women, and young people, from as many of the churches as possible, should informally consider the need for a council. Representatives of existing co-operating organizations should be included. The discussion should take into account the scope and effectiveness of these organizations. Early in the discussion the group should list the community tasks that demand the total resources of the churches working together.

Answer These Ten Questions

This conference should face and find some of the answers to these ten questions:

What is a council of churches? (See Chapter 2.)

What are the needs that churches should face together in our community? (See Chapters 5 and 8.)

How do we do this work together? (See Chapters 5, 6, 9.)

How much can be wisely undertaken now? What are the two or three most important or immediate tasks? What should be our long-range goals?

What resources are now available: In the community—personnel—program? In the state—program and organization, i.e., through your state council and through the National Council? (See Chapter 17.)

What organization is necessary? (See Chapters 3, 5, 10.)

How will it operate? (See Chapters 9, 14.)

How will it be financed? (See Chapter 15.)

Will it be related to other organizations? (See Chapter 13.)

How can we provide for program expansion? (See Chapters 15 and 16.)

Some committees use a blackboard to advantage. Others have a committee prepare brief answers to these questions and mimeograph them for consideration by the group.

Secure as much agreement as possible to the program of work to be recommended. After careful study of the community needs, the local churches must themselves determine what they will do together; the best council programs are made for the community by the churches of the community. Such programs consist of the tasks most necessary and appropriate under local conditions at the time. They also take into account the resources available for the task.

The best advice available will save time; the presence in this and later meetings of a state council or national leader, or of the executive of the council in a nearby city, will prove advantageous.

This conference should appoint an unofficial continuation committee.

The Continuation Committee

The Continuation Committee may have three broad responsibilities to formulate the recommendations of the first conferences so as to

1. work out a plan of organization;
2. work out a constitution;
3. work out a plan of financing.

It may be necessary to hold several meetings of the informal conference group, so as to have them carefully consider the foundation principles of a council of churches (Chapter 3), a plan of organization, and a plan of financing. Next the Continuation Committee should formulate a tentative constitution, using as a basis the constitution and charts in Chapter 5. The plan of organization should allow for growth and expansion, but at the start should include only those departments and committees necessary to meet the immediate needs of program and administration.

Adopt a Plan of Financing

A necessary task of the Continuation Committee will be the formulation of a plan of financing those aspects of the work of each congregation that they wish to carry on through their organization of the council of churches. The committee will have to settle the questions as to whether the work projected can be carried on entirely by volunteers using the facilities of the various churches, whether an office and equipment may be needed, whether a part-time or a full-time secretary will be needed, or (in larger communities) whether an employed executive may be needed. This all points to the need of a budget. "What will it cost?" is one of the first questions that will be asked.

Sample budget requirements for the needs of councils according to size would include some of the following:

Volunteer Council

Program projects	Postage
(including union services)	Publicity
Secretarial services	Printing
Mimeographing	Supplies

Small Council with Full-time Executives

Salaries	Rent
Social Security and retirement	Telephone

Travel	Division of Christian Education
Utilities	Division of Life and Work
Office expense	Division of Christian Missions
Monthly bulletin	United Church Women
Annual meeting	United Church Men
Periodicals and literature	United Youth Fellowship
Convention	United Ministerial Fellowship
Publicity	Radio and television

Larger Council with Employed Personnel

Employed personnel	Program expenses
Salaries	Division of Christian Education
Retirement	Division of Life and Work
Travel	Division of Christian Missions
Hospital chaplaincy	United Church Women
Office expenses	United Church Men
Rent	United Youth Fellowship
Telephone	United Ministerial Fellowship
Office supplies	Radio and television
Office equipment	Conferences (delegates)
Promotion expense	Holy Week services
Monthly "Reporter"	Public meetings
Postage	Audio-visual
Printing	Community school
Publicity	Wider work
Literature	Unbudgeted income
Fund-raising	(See Chapters 15 and 17 for further suggestions).

Next, the sources of income will need to be analyzed; and this will involve the method of securing the underwriting of the budget by the co-operating churches. After the possible methods suggested in Chapter 15 have been discussed in the informal conference and a tentative budget worked out by the committee, the Continuation Committee, or a special subcommittee on finances, should work out a plan for the underwriting of the budget. It will be best to call a meeting of the pastor and chairman of the official board, vestry, session, or trustees of each local church, to explain the plan of the council and discuss the method of financing.

If by this time there is some clear idea of the special services the council might undertake, a simple flip chart to explain these areas of work will help these leaders to visualize what aspects of their churches' program the council will undertake.

After all these elements have been considered and worked into a tentative constitution, the Continuation Committee should formally convene the pastors and two or more elected lay representatives from each interested church to consider the constitution. These delegates should not attempt to take official action for their respective churches, but should discuss, suggest changes if necessary, then approve in principle the tentative constitution, and agree to refer it to the churches.

Refer the Constitution to the Churches

When the proposed constitution has thus been approved in principle, it should be referred by the Continuation Committee to the official body of each church (session, vestry, official board, or congregation). Arrangements should be made to explain the details to each such official group. In each church the Continuation Committee should secure the *official approval* of the church, and the official appointment of its delegates to the council. This process may take several months.

Call a Constituting Meeting

When the Continuation Committee believes that enough churches to insure sufficient strength to carry out the program have officially voted to join the council, the committee should convene the official delegates of the churches. At this meeting the committee should offer a tentative budget that will show the willingness of the several churches to assume their fair share of the cost of their work that they plan to carry on co-operatively, and should nominate the officers of the council. (See Chapter 6.)

The Organizing Session

A properly called meeting of the delegates, proceeding under the constitution approved by their several churches, should then elect the officers, department heads, and committee chairmen of the council. This initial personnel should be chosen with the greatest care. Their good standing, sound sense, administrative ability, patience, tact, and other leadership qualities will be invaluable. An established council can perhaps get on after a fashion with a weak administration; but a new one positively *must* have the best leadership available. Even in smaller communities that are dependent on volunteer leaders, some one person, preferably the president or the secretary, must do earnest and continuous thinking in terms of the whole community. In a city of even moderate size, at least a part-time secretary is needed. In a large city the council of churches demands the skilled and continuous leadership of a full-time executive with secretarial help.

It should be understood that no financial obligations will be assumed until there are resources to meet them. Experience has shown the wisdom of underwriting the initial costs for at least a year in advance of incurring them—the whole future of the council could easily be imperiled if it ran up bills it could not pay promptly. If there is rent to be paid, and personnel to be employed, the council must be sure of the money to meet a reasonable number of paydays before it signs contracts. Neither landlord nor secretary ought to be expected to carry personally what is really the corporate responsibility of the co-operating churches. In larger places it will be advisable to organize in such a manner as to permit early incorporation without the necessity for radical reorganization.

Though these eleven suggested steps may seem like a long process, the experience of the years has shown clearly that, especially in larger communities, only such careful, patient planning and procedure can secure the sound organization that alone means permanence. The first few months can make or break a council; a good start will prove half the battle.

Chapter 5

CONSTITUTIONS
· ·

J. Quinter Miller

Type One:

City, County, or Trade Area

This sample constitution makes provision for Christian co-operation in larger cities, counties, or trade areas. Larger cities are those of 100,000 or more, "Trade areas" is a phrase that covers population groups drawn together by such common interests as trade, communication, recreation, or education; though such areas may cut across state lines or other political subdivisions. (The figures used are only suggestive, and should be adapted to the needs of the specific communities.)

Sample Constitution

Preamble

In the Providence of God, the time has come when it seems fitting more fully to manifest our oneness in Jesus Christ as Divine Lord and Savior, by the creation of an inclusive co-operative agency of the Christian churches of_____

_____

(name of the city, county, or trade area to be included in the council)

ARTICLE I. *Organization and Name*

There shall be an organization that shall be called the _____
Council of the Churches of Christ hereinafter referred to as "the Council."

ARTICLE II. *Purposes*

The purposes of the Council are:

1. To manifest the common spirit and purpose of the co-operating churches in carrying out their mission in the community and the world.
2. To do for the churches such co-operative work as they authorize the Council to carry on in their behalf. This may include work in Christian education, Christian life and work, Christian missions, evangelism, stewardship, broadcasting and films, planning and adjustment in matters of church extension, and such other service as may achieve more effectively the objectives of the Christian religion.

34

3. To encourage fellowship and mutual counsel concerning the spiritual life and religious activities of the churches.
4. To study the religious needs of the community and devise plans to meet these needs.
5. To maintain fellowship and co-operation with other councils of churches throughout the world that, by the action of their highest constitutional authority, are in agreement with the Preamble of this Constitution.

ARTICLE III. *Membership*

1. Local congregations that accept the purpose of this Council as set forth in this Preamble and Constitution are eligible to membership in this Council.
2. The Council may name as affiliated bodies other moral and religious organizations within the community that have a Christian purpose, even if they do not qualify as evangelical churches. Such affiliation is for the purpose of providing an advisory, consultative, or co-operative relationship in the Council Assembly in such numbers as the Council shall determine, but without the power to vote.

ARTICLE IV. *Council Assembly*

1. The governing body of the Council shall be an assembly. Each congregation that has membership in the Council shall be entitled to representation in the Assembly as follows:
   a. Five representatives, to include a minister, a layman, a laywoman, and a young person.
   b. One additional representative for each 300 members or major fraction thereof; and above the first 300, equally divided as far as possible among laymen, laywomen, and young people.
   c. These representatives shall be elected by each member church, and certified to the Assembly by the proper authority of the church.
2. Resident officials of each co-operating communion shall be invited to be members of the Assembly, ex officio.
3. The officers of the Council and the chairmen of its divisions, general departments, and central departments shall be additional representatives in the Assembly.
4. The Assembly shall meet at least three times a year, one meeting being the annual meeting.
5. Thirty-five persons shall constitute a quorum.

ARTICLE V. *Functions of the Council Assembly*

The functions of the Assembly shall include:

1. The general oversight and co-ordination of the whole field of work of the Council, and of its divisions, departments, and committees.
2. Responsibility for all actions and utterances of the Council in its representation of the co-operating churches.

3. The authorization of basic studies in the fields of common interest to the member churches.
4. General control of the financial and business operations of the Council.
5. The election of officers, and chairmen of divisions, departments, and committees.

ARTICLE VI. *Officers of the Council*

1. The officers of the Council shall be a president and at least two vice-presidents—one a woman, a recording secretary, and a treasurer. They shall perform the usual duties of their respective offices, and shall serve until their successors are elected.
2. Persons for these offices shall be nominated from the Council membership by the Nominating Committee, and elected for terms of two years.
3. No officer may serve more than two terms consecutively.
4. The treasurer shall be bonded in an amount fixed by the Board of Directors.
5. Any vacancies occurring between annual meetings shall be filled by the Board of Directors.

ARTICLE VII. *Board of Directors*

1. The Council shall have a board of directors, consisting of the officers of the Council, the chairmen of the divisions, the general departments, and the central departments, and one Assembly member designated by each communion, and presented by the Nominating Committee for election by the Assembly at its annual meeting. Each member of the Board must be a member in good standing of a church that is a constituent member of the Council.
2. The Board shall have the full powers of the Council ad interim except the power to determine the membership of the Council, and the power to revise its Constitution. The Board may appoint such committees as may be necessary.
3. The Board shall recommend to the Council at its annual meeting a program of activities and a budget for the ensuing year.
4. The Board shall appoint all members of divisions, departments of divisions, and central departments.
5. The Board shall meet at least three times a year.
6. Fifteen persons shall constitute a quorum.

ARTICLE VIII. *Executive Committee*

1. The Executive Committee shall consist of the officers of the Council, plus five members at large elected by the Board from its membership, with due regard for the adequate representation of ministers, laymen, laywomen, and young people.
2. This Executive Committee shall be administrative in function, and shall advise the staff and officers in their carrying out the actions of the Assembly and the Board of Directors.

ARTICLE IX. *Program Divisions*

1. The Council shall constitute three program divisions, the distinctions among which are broadly functional as follows:
   a. Division of Christian Education
   b. Division of Christian Life and Work
   c. Division of Christian Missions
2. Each division shall have primary responsibility for developing programs and procedures in its own field, and may recommend to the Board the establishment of such program departments as the needs in its field may require.
3. Chairmen of divisions shall be elected by the Assembly for a period of two years, on nomination of the Nominating Committee.
4. Program Division personnel shall consist of the division chairman, the chairmen of such program departments within each division as are provided in the Bylaws, and representatives from the Assembly and general departments, assigned in such manner as the Council shall determine, seeking as far as possible to assign each representative in accord with his special interest.

ARTICLE X. *General Departments*

1. The Council shall make provision for such general departments as the needs of Christian fellowship require, including
   a. United Ministerial Fellowship
   b. United Church Men
   c. United Church Women*
   d. United Christian Youth
2. Each general department shall have primary responsibility for the development of Christian fellowship, the interpretation of the work of the Council, and the development of program projects within its own field.
3. The personnel of the general departments shall be selected from their co-operating congregations and other co-operating organizations. When such persons are selected from organizations or congregations not in agreement with the Preamble of this Constitution, their participation shall be consultative and advisory, without the power to vote.
4. Each general department shall have the responsibility of electing its own officers, determining its organization, structure, program, and budget operations. (For sample constitutions confer with the corresponding general department of the National Council.)

ARTICLE XI. *Central Departments*

1. The Council shall constitute a Central Department of Business and

---

* Wherever there is a council of United Church Women, it shall, if mutually agreed, become the General Department of United Church Women. In such cases a member of this general department shall be a member of the Central Department of Business and Finance.

Finance, consisting of a chairman, the treasurer, and not fewer than seven others, the purpose of which shall be:

    a. To develop and supervise a program for securing gifts and appropriations essential to the long-term well-being and support of the current budget of the Council.

    b. To cultivate support from congregations, corporations, foundations, and individuals.

    c. To prepare the annual budget for submission to the Board of Directors, and on approval by the Assembly, to supervise all budget operations.

    d. To provide those treasury and business services that may be required.

    e. To provide for an annual audit of the financial records of the Council by a C.P.A.

2. The Council shall constitute a Central Department of Public Relations, consisting of a chairman and not fewer than six others who have competence in the use of such media as press, radio, television, or films, the purpose of which shall be:

    a. To assist the churches in their presentation of the Christian Gospel by means of public relations media and techniques.

    b. To create a better understanding by the general public of the cooperative work of the churches.

    c. To develop the Council's public relations program in the use of newspapers, radio, television, films, audio-visual aids, printed material, exhibits, and advertising, in such a way as to advance every phase of the Council's program.

ARTICLE XII. *Nominating Committee*

1. The Council shall constitute a standing nominating committee of five persons, on nomination of the Executive Committee, each member of which shall be from a different denomination. Due regard to continuity and rotation shall be given in the selection of the membership of this committee.

2. The duties of this committee are to nominate

    a. The officers of the Council.

    b. The chairmen of divisions, central departments, and such departments and standing committees as may be appointed by the Board of Directors.

    c. Communion representatives on the Board of Directors.

    d. Three members at large to the Executive Committee.

    e. All other nominations that are the responsibility of the Board, including the personnel of divisions, departments of divisions, and central departments.

3. This committee shall present to the Assembly for confirmation the names of the officers elected by the general departments.

ARTICLE XIII. *Staff*

The Council shall have an executive secretary and such other personnel as may be required.

ARTICLE XIV. *Financial Support*

The financial support of the Council shall be primarily the responsibility of the bodies that are members of the Council.

ARTICLE XV. *Amendments*

This Constitution may be amended at any meeting of the Assembly by a majority vote of the members present, provided that written notice of such amendment shall have been given to all members at least thirty (30) days in advance of the meeting.

ARTICLE XVI. *Relationships*

The Council shall function locally as an auxiliary of the state council of churches, and shall participate in the development of its programs. Through the state council, it shall be affiliated with the National Council of the Churches of Christ in the United States of America. Its budget shall include annual contributions to the state council and the National Council.

ARTICLE XVII. *Bylaws*

The Council may adopt such bylaws as it deems proper, provided they are not in conflict with this Constitution.

Sample General Bylaws
ARTICLE I. *Record of Membership*

The recording secretary shall keep an up-to-date roll of the local congregations that are members of the Council, according to the provisions of Article III, Section 1, of the Constitution, and of the affiliated organizations according to Article III, Section 2, of the Constitution.

ARTICLE II. *Enrollments*

1. The executive secretary shall advise the local congregations that are entitled to representation in the Assembly regarding these privileges, and shall compile the roll of those representatives to the Assembly who have been certified by the member congregations.
2. Representatives from local congregations to the Assembly shall be appointed for two-year terms, beginning at the time of the meeting of the Assembly subsequent to their election and continuing until their successors are appointed.

ARTICLE III. *Membership Committee*

The Council shall appoint a constituent membership committee, consisting of a chairman and two others, who shall provide biennially full information regarding Council membership and representation in its Assembly, and regarding applications for membership and representation as provided in Articles I and II of these Bylaws.

ARTICLE IV.   *Departments of Program Divisions*

The Board of Directors may appoint such departments within the three program divisions as the needs of the Council may require. The persons so named shall as far as possible be from among those responsible for similar work within the member congregations and communions. These program departments may include:

1. Division of Christian Education
    a. The Religious Education of Children
    b. The Religious Education of Youth
    c. The Religious Education of Adults
    d. Leadership Training
    e. Christian Family Life
    f. Audio-Visual Education
    g. Vacation Church Schools
    h. Weekday Church Schools

2. Division of Christian Life and Work
    a. Evangelism and Worship
    b. Christian Social Relations
        (1) The Church and Economic Life
        (2) Legislative Action
        (3) Liquor Control
        (4) Racial and Cultural Relations
        (5) International Affairs
    c. Ministry in Institutions
    d. Pastoral Services
    e. Social Welfare
    f. Stewardship and Benevolence

3. Division of Christian Missions
    a. Friendly Relations among Foreign Students
    b. Ministry to Migrants
    c. Missionary Education
    d. Church Planning and Adjustment
    e. Church World Service

ARTICLE V.   *Executive Staff*

1. The Board of Directors shall employ an executive secretary and fix the salary and term of office. The executive secretary shall be the executive officer of the Council and a member, ex officio, of all its units, without the power to vote.
2. The Board of Directors may employ such additional staff members as may be required, and shall fix the salary and term of office of each.

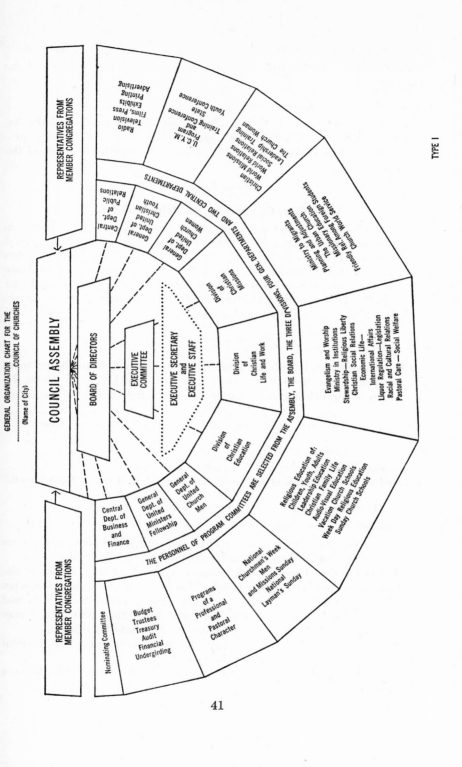

TYPE I

41

Article VI. *Conduct of Meetings*

Robert's *Rules of Order* shall be the official rules of order for all units of the Council.

Article VII. *Amendments*

These general Bylaws may be amended at any regular meeting of the Assembly by a two-thirds vote of the representatives present and voting, provided that written notice shall have been sent out as part of the call of the meeting.

Type Two:

Small City, Community, or Neighborhood

This sample constitution makes provision for Christian co-operation in small cities and communities (less than 100,000). It is intended to suggest a simple pattern that may be adapted to the needs of small groups of churches that wish to work together on common tasks. Where more detailed guidance is desired, adaptations may be made from the sample constitution for larger cities suggested in Type One. (The figures used are only suggestive and should be adapted to the needs of the specific community.)

Sample Constitution

Preamble

In the Providence of God, the time has come when it seems fitting more fully to manifest our oneness in Jesus Christ as Divine Lord and Savior, by the creation of an inclusive co-operative agency of the Christian churches of

_____

(name of the city, community, or neighborhood included in the Council)

Article I. *Organization and Name*

There shall be an organization that shall be called the_____
Council of the Churches of Christ, hereinafter referred to as "the Council."

Article II. *Purposes*

The purposes of the Council are:

1. To manifest the common spirit and purpose of the co-operating churches in carrying out their mission in the community and the world.
2. To do for the churches such co-operative work as they authorize the Council to carry on in their behalf. This may include work in Christian education, Christian life and work, Christian missions, evangelism, and stewardship, broadcasting and films, and such other activities as may more effectively achieve the objectives of the Christian religion.
3. To encourage fellowship and mutual counsel concerning the spiritual life and religious activities of the churches.
4. To study the religious needs of the community and devise plans to meet those needs.

5. To maintain fellowship and co-operation with other councils of churches throughout the world that, by action of their highest constitutional authority, are in agreement with the Preamble of this Constitution.

ARTICLE III. *Membership and Representation*

1. Local congregations that accept the purposes of this Council as set forth in this Preamble and Constitution are eligible to membership in this Council.
2. Each member congregation is entitled to name four representatives to the Assembly of the Council, including a minister, a layman, a lay-woman, and a young person, plus an additional lay person for each 300 members above the first 300.
3. The Assembly shall meet at least twice a year, one meeting being the annual meeting.
4. Twenty-one persons shall constitute a quorum.

ARTICLE IV. *Functions of the Council Assembly*

It is the function of the Assembly of the Council to provide for the general direction, oversight, and co-ordination of the whole field of the work of the Council, its departments and committees, to make provision for and control its financial and business operations, and to elect its officers, departments other than general departments, and committees.

ARTICLE V. *Officers of the Council*

1. The officers shall be a president and at least two vice-presidents—one a woman, a secretary, and a treasurer. They shall perform the usual duties of their respective offices, and shall serve until their successors are elected.
2. Persons for these offices shall be nominated from the Council membership by the Nominating Committee, and elected for terms of two years.
3. Any vacancies occurring between annual meetings shall be filled by the Executive Committee.

ARTICLE VI. *Executive Committee*

1. The Council shall have an executive committee consisting of the officers of the Council and the chairmen of its departments and standing committees.
2. The Executive Committee shall have the full powers of the Council ad interim, except the power to determine the membership of the Council and the power to revise its Constitution. The Executive Committee may appoint such committees as may be necessary.
3. The Executive Committee shall recommend to the Council at its annual meeting a program of activities and a budget for the ensuing year.
4. The Executive Committee shall meet at least three times a year.
5. Seven persons shall constitute a quorum.

ARTICLE VII. *Departments*

1. The Council shall establish such activities as the member churches wish to undertake together. These activities may be organized into:

   a. Program departments, including
      (1) Christian Education
      (2) Christian Life and Work
      (3) Christian Missions
   b. General departments, including
      (1) United Ministerial Fellowship
      (2) United Church Men
      (3) United Church Women*
      (4) United Christian Youth
   c. Central departments, including
      (1) Business and Finance
      (2) Radio and Television
      (3) Public Relations

2. Program departments shall consist of a chairman, and one person from each of the fields of interest included in the functions of the department, and representatives of the Assembly assigned in such manner as the Council shall determine, seeking as far as possible to assign each representative according to his particular interest.

3. Each general department shall have primary responsibility for the development of Christian fellowship, the interpretation of the work of the Council, and the development of program projects within its own field, selecting its own officers, and the determining of its form of organization, program, and budget operations.

4. Each central department shall consist of a chairman, and not fewer than five persons appointed by the Council because of their special competence in the work of the specific central departments.

ARTICLE VIII. *Nominating Committee*

1. The Council shall elect a nominating committee consisting of three persons, on nomination of the Executive Committee, no two of whom shall be from the same denomination.

2. The duties of this committee are to nominate the officers of the Council and the chairmen of the program departments, central departments, and committees.

3. This committee shall present to the annual meeting for confirmation the names of the officers elected by the general departments.

---

* Wherever there is a council of United Church Women, it shall, if mutually agreed, become the General Department of United Church Women. In such cases a member of this general department shall be a member of the Central Department of Business and Finance.

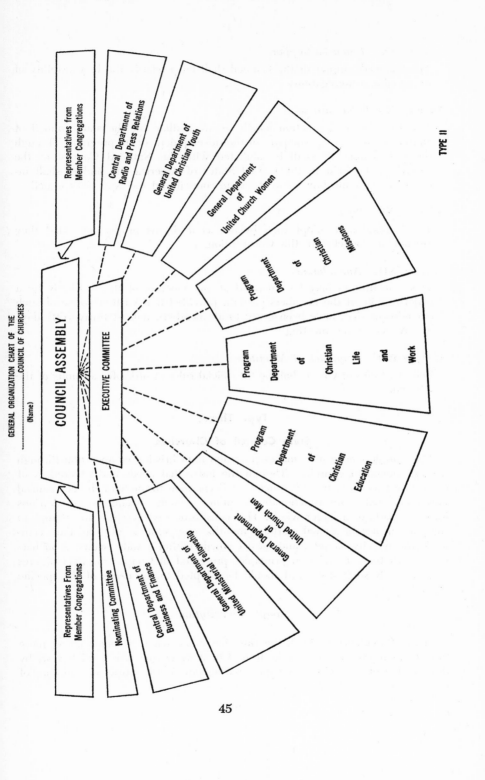

GENERAL ORGANIZATION CHART OF THE
..................COUNCIL OF CHURCHES
(Name)

COUNCIL ASSEMBLY

EXECUTIVE COMMITTEE

Representatives from
Member Congregations

Representatives From
Member Congregations

Central Department of
Radio and Press Relations

General Department of
United Christian Youth

General Department
of
United Church Women

Program
Department
of
Christian
Missions

Program
Department
of
Christian
Life
and
Work

Program
Department
of
Christian
Education

General Department
of
United Church Men

United Ministerial Fellowship

Central Department of
Business and Finance

Nominating Committee

TYPE II

45

ARTICLE IX. *Financial Support*

The financial support of the Council shall be primarily the responsibility of its member congregations.

ARTICLE X. *Relationships*

This Council shall function locally as an auxiliary of the state council of churches, and shall participate in the development of its program. Through the state council it shall be affiliated with the National Council of the Churches of Christ in the United States of America. Its budget shall include annual contributions to the state council and the National Council.

ARTICLE XI. *Bylaws*

The Council may adopt such bylaws as it deems proper, provided they are not in conflict with this Constitution.

ARTICLE XII. *Amendments*

This Constitution may be amended at any meeting of the Assembly by a majority vote of the members present, provided that written notice of such amendment shall have been given to all members at least thirty (30) days in advance of the meeting.

ARTICLE XIII. *Conduct of Meetings*

Robert's *Rules of Order* shall be the official rules of order for all units of the Council.

Type Three:

State Council of Churches

This sample constitution makes provision for Christian co-operation through a state council of churches. Though the individual needs and differences of each state may vary, there is much that is common throughout the ecumenical movement that helps functionally to unite councils of churches on various levels as parts of a larger whole. This constitution is therefore an attempt to suggest an organizational pattern for the co-operation of Christian communions and city, county, and local councils within a state, which is in harmony with those foundation principles presented in Chapter 3. (The figures used are only suggestive, and should be adapted to the needs of the specific states.)

Sample Constitution

Preamble

In the Providence of God, the time has come when it seems fitting more fully to manifest our oneness in Jesus Christ as Divine Lord and Savior, by the creation of an inclusive co-operative agency of the Christian churches of the state of _____.

ARTICLE I. *Organization and Name*

There shall be an organization that shall be called the _____
(name of state)
Council of the Churches of Christ, hereinafter referred to as "the Council."

ARTICLE II. *Purposes*

The purposes of the Council are:

1. To manifest the common spirit and purpose of the co-operating communions and interdenominational territorial or local units in carrying out their mission in the state, the nation, and the world.
2. To do for the churches such co-operative work as they authorize the Council to carry on in their behalf. This may include work in Christian education, Christian life and work, Christian missions and service, Christian evangelism and stewardship, broadcasting and films, planning and adjustment in matters of church extension, ministry in institutions, and such other service as may achieve more effectively the objectives of the Christian religion.
3. To encourage fellowship and mutual counsel concerning the spiritual life and religious activities of the churches.
4. To study the religious needs of the state and devise plans to meet these needs.
5. To encourage the study of the Bible and to assist in the spread of the Christian religion.
6. To promote co-operation among local churches, and to further in cities, counties, and trade areas the development of interdenominational territorial units in agreement with the Preamble of this Constitution.
7. To maintain fellowship and co-operation with other councils of churches throughout the nation and the world, that by the action of their highest constitutional authority are in agreement with the Preamble of this Constitution.

ARTICLE III. *Membership*

1. Communions that accept the purpose of this Council as set forth in this Preamble and Constitution are eligible to membership in this Council.
2. The Council may name as affiliated bodies other moral and religious organizations within the state that have a Christian purpose, even if they do not qualify as evangelical communions. Such affiliation is for the purpose of providing an advisory, consultative, or co-operative relationship in the Council Assembly in such numbers as the Council shall determine, but without the power to vote.

ARTICLE IV. *Council Assembly*

1. The governing body of the Council shall be an assembly. Representation in the assembly shall be as follows:
   a. Each communion that has membership in the Council shall be en-

titled to appoint five representatives, and one additional representative for every 10,000 of its communicants or major fraction thereof, with due regard to the adequate representation of ministers, laymen, laywomen, and young people.

b. Each interdenominational territorial unit that, by action of its highest constitutional authority, has declared itself to be in agreement with the Preamble of this Constitution and is constituted by the local congregations in its area, shall be entitled to appoint one representative, and one additional representative for every 20,000 communicant church members or major fraction thereof, with due regard to the adequate representation of ministers, laymen, laywomen, and young people.

c. These representatives, having been elected by the appropriate body, shall be certified to the Assembly by the proper authority of the member communion or council.

2. The officers of the Council, the chairmen of its divisions, general departments, and central departments, and members of the General Assembly of the National Council of Churches within the state, shall be additional representatives in the Council Assembly on approval by the communions.

3. The Assembly shall meet annually, on call of the Board of Directors, at a time and place determined by the Board.

4. Thirty-five persons shall constitute a quorum.

ARTICLE V. *Functions of the Council Assembly*

The functions of the Assembly shall include:

1. The general oversight and co-ordination of the whole field of work of the Council, and of its divisions, departments, and committees.

2. Responsibility for all actions and utterances of the Council in its representation of the co-operating churches.

3. The authorization of basic studies in the fields of common interest to the member churches.

4. General control of the financial and business operations of the Council.

5. Election of officers and chairmen of divisions, central departments, and committees.

ARTICLE VI. *Officers of the Council*

1. The officers of the Council shall be a president and at least two vice-presidents—one a woman, a recording secretary, and a treasurer. They shall perform the usual duties of their respective offices, and shall serve until their successors are elected.

2. Persons for these offices shall be nominated from the Council membership by the Nominating Committee, and elected for terms of two years.

3. No officer may serve more than two terms consecutively.

4. The treasurer shall be bonded in an amount fixed by the Board of Directors.
5. Any vacancies occurring between annual meetings shall be filled by the Board of Directors.

ARTICLE VII. *Board of Directors*
1. The Council shall have a Board of Directors consisting of
   a. One-seventh of the number of the representatives named by each member communion to the Council Assembly, with due regard to the adequate representation of ministers, laymen, laywomen, and young people.
   b. One-seventh of the number of representatives appointed by the interdenominational territorial units, with due regard to the adequate representation of ministers, laymen, laywomen, and young people.
   c. One communion executive named by each member communion, not otherwise provided for in Section 1 a) above.
   d. The officers of the Council, and the chairmen of divisions and general and central departments.
   e. Each member of the Board must be a member in good standing of a communion that is a member of the Council.
2. The Board shall have the full powers of the Council ad interim except the power to determine the membership of the Council, and the power to revise its Constitution. The Board may appoint such committees as may be necessary.
3. The Board shall recommend to the Council at its annual meeting a program of activities and a budget for the ensuing year.
4. The Board shall appoint all members of divisions, departments of divisions, and central departments.
5. The Board shall meet not less than twice a year.
6. Twenty-one persons shall constitute a quorum.

ARTICLE VIII. *Executive Committee*
1. The Executive Committee shall consist of the officers of the Council, plus five members at large elected by the Board of Directors from its membership, with due regard for the adequate representation of ministers, laymen, laywomen, and young people.
2. This Executive Committee shall be administrative in function, and shall advise the staff and officers in carrying out the actions of the Assembly and the Board of Directors.

ARTICLE IX. *Program Divisions*
1. The Council shall constitute three program divisions, the distinctions among which are broadly functional as follows:
   a. Division of Christian Education
   b. Division of Christian Life and Work
   c. Division of Christian Missions

2. Each division shall have primary responsibility for developing programs and procedures in its own field, and may recommend to the Board of Directors the establishment of such program departments as the needs of its field may call for.
3. Chairmen of divisions shall be elected by the Assembly for a period of two years, on nomination of the Nominating Committee.
4. Program Division personnel shall consist of the Division chairman, the chairmen of such program departments within each division as are provided in the bylaws, and representatives from the Assembly and general departments, assigned in accord with their special interest and responsibilities.

ARTICLE X. *General Departments*

1. The Council shall make provision for such general departments as the needs of Christian fellowship require, including
   a. United Ministerial Fellowship
   b. United Church Men
   c. United Church Women*
   d. United Christian Youth
2. Each general department shall have primary responsibility for the development of Christian fellowship, the interpretation of the work of the Council, and the development of program projects within its own field.
3. The personnel of the general departments shall be selected from the member communions and other co-operating organizations. When such persons are selected from communions or organizations not in agreement with the Preamble of this Constitution, their participation shall be consultative, without the power to vote.
4. Each general department shall have the responsibility of electing its own officers, determining its organizational structure, program, and budget operations. (For sample constitutions confer with the corresponding general department of the National Council.)

ARTICLE XI. *Central Departments*

1. The Council shall constitute a Central Department of Business and Finance, consisting of a chairman, the treasurer, and not fewer than seven others, the purpose of which shall be:
   a. To develop and supervise a program for securing gifts and appropriations essential to the long-term well-being and support of the current budget of the Council.
   b. To cultivate support from communions, congregations, corporations, foundations, and individuals.

---

* Wherever there is a state council of United Church Women, it shall, if mutually agreed, become the General Department of United Church Women. In such cases a member of this general department shall be a member of the Central Department of Business and Finance.

c. To prepare the annual budget for submission to the Board of Directors, and on approval by the Assembly, to supervise all budget operations.

d. To provide those treasury and business services that may be required.

e. To provide for an annual audit of the financial records of the Council by a C.P.A.

2. The Council shall constitute a Central Department of Public Relations, consisting of a chairman and not fewer than six others who have competence in the use of such media as press, radio, television, or films, the purpose of which shall be:

a. To help the churches in their presentation of the Christian Gospel by means of public relations media and techniques.

b. To create a better understanding by the general public of the co-operative work of the churches.

c. To develop the Council's public relations program in the use of newspapers, radio, television, films, audio-visual aids, printed material, exhibits, and advertising, in such ways as to advance every phase of the Council's program.

ARTICLE XII. *Nominating Committee*

1. The Council shall constitute a standing nominating committee of five persons, on nomination of the Executive Committee, each member of which shall be from a different denomination. Due regard to continuity and rotation shall be given in the selection of members of the committees.

2. The duties of this committee are to nominate

a. The officers of the Council.

b. The chairmen of divisions, central departments, and such departments and standing committees as may be appointed by the Board of Directors.

c. Five members at large to the Executive Committee.

d. All nominations that are the responsibility of the Board of Directors, including the personnel of divisions, departments of divisions, and central departments.

3. This committee shall present to the Assembly for confirmation the names of the officers elected by the general departments.

ARTICLE XIII. *Staff*

The Council shall have an executive secretary, and such other personnel as it may need.

ARTICLE XIV. *Financial Support*

The financial support of the Council shall be primarily the responsibility of the bodies that are members of the Council.

ARTICLE XV. *Amendments*

This Constitution may be amended at any meeting of the Assembly by a majority vote of the members present, provided that written notice of such amendment shall have been given to all members at least thirty (30) days in advance of the meeting.

ARTICLE XVI. *Relationships*

The Council shall be affiliated with the National Council of the Churches of Christ in the United States of America by participation in the development of its program and by contributing annually to its budget.

ARTICLE XVII. *Bylaws*

The Council may adopt such bylaws as it deems proper, provided they are not in conflict with this Constitution.

Sample General Bylaws

ARTICLE I. *Record of Membership*

The recording secretary shall keep an up-to-date roll of the communions that are members, and of the city and county councils that are represented in the Assembly and Board of Directors, according to the provisions of Article III, Article IV, and Article VII of the Constitution.

ARTICLE II. *Enrollments*

The executive secretary shall advise the communions and councils that are entitled to representation in the Assembly regarding these privileges, and shall compile the roll of representatives to the Assembly who have been certified by the member communions and affiliated councils of churches.

ARTICLE III. *Membership Committee*

The Council shall appoint a constituent membership committee, consisting of a chairman and two others, who shall provide biennially full information regarding Council membership and representation in its Assembly, and regarding applications for membership and representation as provided in Articles I and II of these Bylaws.

ARTICLE IV. *Committees of Program Divisions*

The Board of Directors may appoint such departments within the three program divisions as the needs of the Council may require. The persons so named shall as far as possible be from among those responsible for similar work in the member congregations and communions. These program departments may include:

1. Division of Christian Education
   a. The Religious Education of Children
   b. The Religious Education of Youth

    c. The Religious Education of Adults

    d. Leadership Training

    e. Christian Family Life

    f. Audio-Visual Education

    g. Vacation Church Schools

    h. Weekday Church Schools

2. Division of Christian Life and Work

    a. Evangelism and Worship

    b. Christian Social Relations

        (1) The Church and Economic Life

        (2) Legislative Action

        (3) Liquor Control

        (4) Racial and Cultural Relations

        (5) International Affairs

    c. Ministry in Institutions

    d. Pastoral Services

    e. Social Welfare

    f. Stewardship and Benevolence

3. Division of Christian Missions

    a. Friendly Relations among Foreign Students

    b. Ministry to Migrants

    c. Missionary Education

    d. Church Planning and Adjustment

    e. Town and Country Church

    f. Urban Church

    g. Church World Service

ARTICLE V. *Executive Staff*

1. The Board of Directors shall employ an executive secretary and fix the salary and term of office. The executive secretary shall be the executive officer of the Council and a member ex officio of all its units but without the power to vote.

2. The Board of Directors may employ such additional staff members as may be needed, and shall fix the salary and term of office of each.

ARTICLE VI. *Conduct of Meetings*

Robert's *Rules of Order* shall be the official rules of order for all units of the Council.

ARTICLE VII. *Amendments*

These Bylaws may be amended at any regular meeting of the Assembly by a two-thirds vote of the representatives present and voting, provided that written notice shall have been sent out at the time of the call for the meeting.

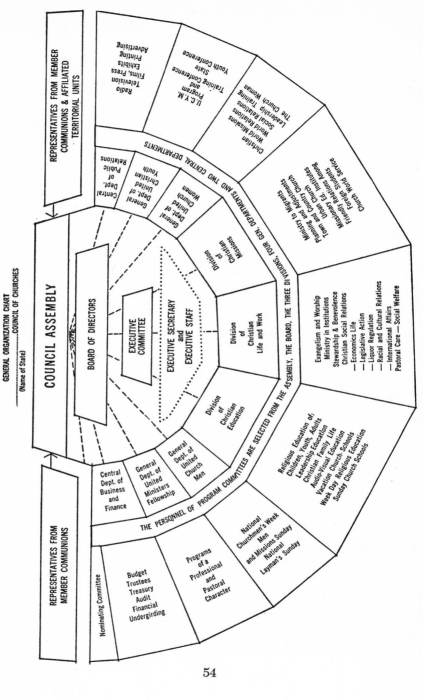

GENERAL ORGANIZATION CHART
............................COUNCIL OF CHURCHES
(Name of State)

TYPE III

REPRESENTATIVES FROM MEMBER COMMUNIONS & AFFILIATED TERRITORIAL UNITS

REPRESENTATIVES FROM MEMBER COMMUNIONS

COUNCIL ASSEMBLY

BOARD OF DIRECTORS

EXECUTIVE COMMITTEE

EXECUTIVE SECRETARY and EXECUTIVE STAFF

Radio
Television
Films, Press
Exhibits
Printing
Advertising

U.C.Y.M.
Program
and
Training Conference
State
Youth Conference

Christian
World Missions
Social Relations
Leadership Training
The Church Woman

Central
Dept.
of
Public
Relations

General
Dept. of
Christian
Youth

General
Dept. of
United
Church
Women

Division
of
Christian
Missions

Planning and Co. Church
Community and Church
Town and Country
Union Ch. and Inst.
Ministry to Migrants
Missionary Education
Missions Research and Adjustments
Ch. Ed. Among Sponsored Missions
Friendly Relations
Foreign World Service
Church

Division
of
Christian
Life and Work

Evangelism and Worship
Ministry in Institutions
Stewardship & Benevolence
Christian Social Relations
— Economics Life
— Legislative Action
— Liquor Regulation
— Racial and Cultural Relations
— International Affairs
Pastoral Care — Social Welfare

Division
of
Christian
Education

Religious Education of:
Children, Youth, Adults
Leadership Education
Christian Family Life
Audio-Visual Education
Vacation Church Schools
Week Day Religious Education
Sunday Church Schools

Central
Dept. of
Business
and
Finance

General
Dept. of
United
Ministers
Fellowship

General
Dept. of
United
Church
Men

Nominating Committee

Budget
Trustees
Treasury
Audit
Financial
Undergirding

Programs
of a
Professional
and
Pastoral
Character

National
Churchmen's Week
Men
and Missions Sunday
National
Layman's Sunday

TWO CENTRAL DEPARTMENTS

FOUR DEPARTMENTS AND TWO CENTRAL DEPARTMENTS

THE PERSONNEL OF PROGRAM COMMITTEES ARE SELECTED FROM THE ASSEMBLY, THE BOARD, THE THREE DIVISIONS, FOUR DEPARTMENTS

54

Chapter 6

PERSONNEL FOR BOARDS AND COMMITTEES

. . . .

G. Merrill Lenox

Due Esteem for Your Cause

To plead the fundamental importance of having an adequate supply of competent personnel for co-operative Christian activities is not the purpose of this chapter—this need is taken for granted. The assignment here, then, is what? To pass along helpful hints for enlisting able voluntary leadership for ecumenical tasks.

The first step in obtaining competent personnel is for the executive to make certain in his own mind that he has placed a high enough valuation on the cause he serves. No man should "think of himself more highly than he ought to think" (Rom. 12:3), but every ecumenical leader should think of *his mission* in the highest terms. Christian unity is a cause after our Lord's own heart. It was the subject of his earnest prayer not long before he was crucified. Unless the ecumenical administrator is convinced that he is engaged in the most important business in the world, he will fail in his search for leaders even before he starts. When he is sure that he has due esteem for his cause, then prayerfully he can face the task of enlisting all the men and women—and the finest—that he needs for its advancement.

The Best Is Not Too Good

Church council work sometimes limps along pathetically when it should be going forward with leaps and bounds, because employed leaders permit themselves to be content with second- or third-rate voluntary leadership. They are tempted to accept leaders left over after local church, denominational, and other community causes have taken their pick. They may plead in their defense that their project is so new that it needs more recognition before they can ask top-flight leaders to enlist. They may rationalize that their organization is still weak, and that it behooves them to be reluctant about asking strong lay leaders and clergy to join their ranks. Or they may have made a valiant attempt to recruit acknowledged leaders, only to be rebuffed. But ecumenical executives must allow no obstacles to discourage them; they must keep their banners flying high. The best of leadership is not too good for their work. "Not failure but low aim is crime" when it comes to the selection of leaders for council activities. If the administrative officials of co-operative church activities have true regard for their cause, they will aspire to the highest in obtaining board and committee personnel.

A Nose for Names

A council executive needs "a nose for names" as much as a reporter needs a nose for news. The administrator should be on the alert for the names of prospective leaders all the time and everywhere. He should have ever present a notebook and a pencil to record promptly every name that comes to his attention. The job of filling the council's many posts will not be well done if the executive depends entirely on having names flash into his mind as he sits down to work at his committee rosters. Scores of able, willing, and devoted prospects will be lost to the effort unless the executive becomes an intrepid name collector. The writer knows at least one board of directors and several strategic committees that have been immeasurably strengthened and enriched by this constant alertness for names. The executive cannot possibly call to mind, when committees are being selected, the scores of individuals who commended themselves to him as prospects in the midst of his myriad activities, unless he has taken pains to record their names.

One does a great deal of thinking about his work as he sits at the wheel of his car. It pays, therefore, to have a heavy piece of cardboard and a pencil on the front seat, to facilitate the immediate jotting down of names (at the next stop light, of course) that occur to him. Many names, and some excellent ideas, have been made a matter of permanent record through this practice of keeping always a handy pencil and pad in one's car.

Filing with a Purpose

After the executive writes down the names, what then? The obvious answer is that he must file them. Now everybody knows that a file can be a burial ground. Many ideas that were vibrantly alive have perished there. The names of many exciting candidates for Christian committee work have vanished for time and eternity in the executive's voluminous files. This need not be—and should not be. Nothing should deter the staff leader from keeping a living, purposeful record of the names of men, women, and youth who might be geared to useful council service. It is not always possible to make an immediate assignment, but the sooner a ready prospect can be challenged to a task, the better. In any case, the file of committee prospects must be considered current and vital, and never relegated to the lost limbo of forgotten records. An orderly file of names of able and available prospects for Christian service might well be the council's greatest single resource for future success.

Approaching the Prospect

If the administrator has due esteem for his cause, what a difference it makes to him whether he gets a "yes" or a "no" answer to his challenge to service in that cause. He approaches his prospect after prayerful planning. He obviously cannot present his case in a personal interview to every person he wants for some aspect of council activity. But he does take time for dignified, convincing personal visits in those cases where the more strategic positions are involved. And he never substitutes a letter for an interview, nor a casual telephone call for a letter, just because he has "let the matter slide," or because he rationalizes that "it doesn't make much difference how you ask a person—just ask him." It makes all the difference in the world. The writer knows of instances where the council constituency has been utterly amazed by affirmative responses to carefully and prayerfully planned requests for Christian leadership. It is obvious that the interviewee will never take more seriously than does his interviewer the task he is asked to assume. Only as the interviewer shows adequate esteem for his cause, and is enough concerned to prepare a sincere and intelligent appeal, can he hope for a favorable response.

When he must appeal by letter, the appeal should be personalized as much as possible, and written with ingenious skill and care. A personal "P.S." to a circular letter improves its chances of an affirmative reply. Skillful telephoning is a technique in itself. The irreducible minimum of diplomacy of course requires that when you call you first find out if the prospect is free to talk, that you keep your message as brief as possible, and that you express your gratitude for whatever past service this potential worker may have given.

It is extremely important to assign the "right" person to get a particular individual's promise to serve. Sometimes it is wise to issue the challenge through a friend, sometimes through the highest executive officer of the organization, and sometimes through someone in his own denomination or someone holding similar views. Scores of effective Christian leaders are in positions of strategic leadership because—and only because—"just the right person" issued the initial challenge to service.

Space is not available here to consider the many other factors that make an interview effective. But it cannot be too much emphasized that persons approached for Christian service are often needlessly lost to the cause by a bungling invitation.

Assign Tasks Commensurate with Ability and Availability

One mistake frequently made in the recruiting of personnel is to assign the enlistee to an inappropriate responsibility. It is important to line up for service as many able and representative leaders as possible, and then to assign to them tasks that are commensurate with their ability and their availability.

There should always be room on council boards and committees for widely known and highly respected persons, even though they may be available only for honorary status. A council's program is markedly strengthened to have such Christian laymen identified with it, even though they may be unable to devote time to the work—and once they are tied in, that time may come. There will also be influential persons who will give large blocks of time and energy if the jobs they are asked to perform are in line with their special interest and ability. To challenge such laymen to serve and then to assign them trifling tasks would be a sure way of forfeiting their interest. Don't let it happen!

Every council must depend in considerable measure on consecrated men, women, and youth of average ability who are "sold" on the cause, and are therefore willing to do anything they can that promises to advance the work. Such "salt of the earth" ecumenical enthusiasts must be utilized to the full. An alert administrator can open avenues of purposeful activity for them all.

For the few community personalities who find it impossible to attend regular committee meetings or follow through on even important assignments, special provision must be made. It is often wise to use their names on sponsors' lists for various events, to have them preside or participate in big meetings, or to use quotations from them in council literature. Many councils have widely known Protestant civic leaders preside at daily Lenten services. The list of such presiders has included mayors, governors, top executives of leading companies, high-ranking labor leaders, administrative heads of denominations, and other luminaries whose names are well known throughout the community. Competent leaders who are willing to render service but who are exceedingly busy in their own vocations will often head ad hoc committees when they might resist standing committee service with its exhausting demands.

If the council executive has due esteem for his high mission, and assigns tasks commensurate with the volunteers' ability and availability, his personnel problem will be well on its way to solution.

Let Your Leaders Lead—Commit to Your Committees

A bank president or other prominent citizen whose name is on a letterhead as a sponsor of some ecumenical project has confidence in the organization, but probably does not expect to be regularly consulted on policy and program. Yet if such a man is challenged to head an important functioning committee and then both he and his committee are ignored, he loses interest in the cause and may desert it altogether. Here is a spot in which an executive must proceed with great wisdom. He must work unobtrusively with his committees, yet must make sure that notices are sent out promptly, agenda are set up, and necessary preparatory material for meetings is provided. But in all this he must of course be certain of the chairman's approval without unduly "pestering" him with trivialities. That is, the executive must guide with skill, but must meticulously refrain from robbing the chairman of his prerogatives. He must let his leaders lead, while he stands close by to inspire and support. A committee on its own without the expert guidance of a diplomatic staff director might well fail. On the other hand, an employed staff member who usurps the leader's position may soon discover he has lost all his most able leaders.

When the administrator is advised to commit jobs to committees, this does not mean that he should forthwith desert those committees and leave them to sink or swim. A committee needs the employed staff worker; and he also needs his committee. He must arrange for committee members to have an ample share in discussions, so that their final decisions will represent the convictions of a significant body, and never the arbitrary dicta of the executive or joint pronouncements by the executive and the chairman.

58

An aggressive administrator is frequently tempted to plunge ahead with his program and override the accepted committee procedures. He may take much too seriously the familiar adage, "If you want a thing well done, do it yourself." But his experience will teach him that the only way for his organization to continue to do many things well is through soundly established and actively functioning committees. The council executive who insists on dominating his committees will ultimately fail. If he considers his volunteers as mere pawns in his hands to accomplish his personal objectives, he will soon have no body of workers.

Vital Program Attracts Vigorous Leaders

The council executive can never escape the hard truth that his only ultimate hope to retain competent personnel lies in the vitality of his program. He can fool all his potential helpers part of the time, and perhaps some of them all the time, but he cannot fool all of them all the time. They will respond to a call for volunteers for a job that produces proof of its current relevance or promise of future significance. But they cannot be hoodwinked for very long into squandering their time and talent in a languishing effort. Therefore the best way for the executive to hold his personnel and recruit new is to operate *through them* a live and creative program.

In this matter of enlisting leaders, it is always refreshing to examine one's practices honestly. If one finds he leans heavily on unsuspecting newcomers to his community, or is almost exclusively bound to a deeply entrenched and unimaginative Old Guard, something surely is wrong. A vital program of activities, and proper practices in securing personnel for it, will hold the confidence of dependable veterans, and also attract able and willing new arrivals.

Personnel That Represents

You no doubt have seen committees composed of outstanding and industrious leaders that obtained only modest success in their work, and you have asked yourself "why?" After you studied the case you probably discovered that the committee members did not officially represent anybody. As isolated individuals they performed superbly; but their committee activities they carried on as in a vacuum. When a council of churches is dependent on communions and individual congregations for the support of its budget and activities, it must have on its committees persons who are representative of those component bodies. For when it studies a problem it needs to have men and women who are in touch with the council's constituency in order to know how that constituency feels about that problem. (See "The Principle of Committee Membership," Chapter 3.) When it is promoting a project that requires general attendance at some assemblage, it must consist of representatives who can effectively arouse interest in the event that is being promoted. If financial undergirding is the desired end, the committee must have official access to the sources of support.

There are of course exceptions. There is room for resourceful specialists or willing and dedicated enthusiasts on certain types of committees. Care should be taken to make the most of such valuable persons. But the representative principle must in general be followed, or the program will inevitably bog down badly and may fail completely.

It Is God's Work

And now back to where this chapter began. There must be in the mind and heart of every council administrator a burning passion for his cause. To him it must be God's work, and his part in it must unmistakably be God's will for his life. He cannot capture anyone else for a cause that has failed to capture him. His greatest asset in procuring competent personnel is therefore his own profound faith in the transcendent significance of his mission, and his prayerful desire to have others share it to the full.

Chapter 7

TRAINING STAFF AND COMMITTEE PERSONNEL
. . . .

E. C. Farnham

The expenditure of thought, time, and effort in the training of staff and committee personnel can prevent many difficulties later and add greatly to the smoothness and efficiency of the whole operation.

The two classifications differ in the approach to their responsibilities, and usually in their background of professional training, and therefore cannot be considered altogether alike in the matter of training. Committee personnel may include those who have professional training in the particular field of interest, or their training may be in kindred fields, or their background may be in a totally different field. Staff personnel, however, are employed because they have professional competence for the particular service to be performed. Staff responsibility also differs from committee responsibility, and therefore the training must be different. Staff personnel who have relations with committees must be conversant with committee training; and committees should have some awareness of staff responsibilities.

Staff Training

Staff training is conditioned by the personnel policies adopted by the board of directors by whom the staff members are employed. Personnel policies may differ among organizations in terms of their particular needs and conditions; therefore these policies cannot be assumed to be general or generally understood. The personnel policy of a particular organization should be worked out with much thought and care, and with a proper regard for the policies of kindred organizations. The policies of the social welfare department of a council of churches should be built on studies of other social welfare organizations of the community; if they aren't, differences in the policies that affect workers of similar professions will become known, and will result in unhappiness, frequent change, and loss of organizational efficiency. The personnel policy should be definite, cover all the essential points of employer-employee relations, and leave as little room as possible for later controversy—of course not in such detail as to affront the intelligence of the person involved. The policy will cover such matters as hours of work, vacation, sick leave, holidays, salary schedule, pension plan, relation to other units in the organization, and a careful description of the work for which the person is being employed.

61

A second element in staff training might be called house rules. The job description should make the clearest possible demarcation of function among the different offices, officers, departments, and programs.

House rules should establish clearly the division of responsibilities and the relations among employees of executive rank. It is important to make clear wherein the staff person has full responsibility, and the point at which his responsibility is limited. Questions of policy and procedure and finance in a particular department may be left to the head of that department, until they become questions that affect the whole organization; then they should be referred to the responsible person or board for decision. There should always be a clear understanding between the employing agency and the employee as to personal working relationships.

House rules should cover the over-all policies, objectives, and procedures of the organization, and the relations of the particular office, person, or department. Since a council is a church organization, how much prominence should be given to the religious note in the work-a-day routines? What is to be the attitude toward antagonistic or nonco-operative elements? Are workers and committees or departments to be creative in their outlook? What procedures are to be followed in dealing with controversial matters that involve a constituency larger than that of the particular committee or department?

House rules that involve executive and professional workers should cover the responsibility for written reports, for attendance at meetings, for sharing in staff conferences, for the representation of the organization in community affairs, for methods and co-operative relationships in the handling of publicity, for relationship to and attendance at meetings of boards of the organization, and whether such attendance is on a voting or nonvoting basis.

How is this instruction accomplished? Obviously, the several points should first be thought out by the agency responsible for employing staff personnel and for their subsequent supervision. As far as possible these points should be written out, with a copy given to the person being employed.

Next come the personal interviews. The first of these is before employment. This must discover the person's preparation and fitness for the work, a description of its objectives and general procedures, and its personnel policies. Conferences after employment should be frequent, either on a fixed time-program or as the occasion prompts. These informal conferences make for the best working relations: mutuality, goodwill, and comradeship are the only true basis for effective Christian service. Consultation among staff members for friendly exchange and the discussion of problems, including the problems of the chief executive, make for goodwill and learning, and help to weld the staff into an effective, powerful team.

Staff conferences are important training media. In large organizations these conferences may be classified: a general staff conference for matters of general interest or concern; an executive staff conference for the consideration of interdepartmental matters; a clerical staff conference to deal with office procedures. In councils of churches it is desirable that all employees have regular opportunity for corporate worship. Such gatherings may provide for a brief period of business—report of matters of common interest, or consideration of a policy, or a new working rule. Such meetings might be chaired by any employee. Staff leaders might take turns in reporting items of activity and interest for their respective departments. Democratic participation makes for morale and team play, both of which are basic objectives of staff training.

Records of earlier activities and reference books should be made available for use by employees. Suggestions for the study of comparable positions and procedures in kindred organizations may prove valuable. Provision should be made for attendance at professional conferences, institutes, or training schools. A staff retreat or setting-up conference for all employees at the opening of the work season or for preparation for a new year, using the better part of a day, or a week end, with a program arranged by a staff committee, can prove invaluable. Conferences on the preparation of the annual report of the organization will contribute to a better understanding of basic considerations.

Personnel in a specialized department, such as social welfare or religious education, may follow methods similar to those of the general staff. Care should be taken that departmental staffs feel themselves to be an integral part of the total general organization. The frequent presence of the chief executive of the organization at departmental staff meetings will help strengthen this consciousness of being a part of the whole. The departmental staff may be asked to present its program in dramatic form for the enjoyment and instruction of the general staff, and thus contribute to the training program. Occasional social affairs will be helpful. The presence at such affairs of members of the board of directors and of officers will add to morale and devotion. And of course the exchange of courtesies and commendation for work well done always makes for good staff relationships.

Training of Committees

Much of the foregoing is equally true in the training of committees. It will help in determining the appropriate program of training, if the organizational structure is clearly defined, particularly as to the scope and range of its responsibility. One scheme of classification may include a division covering a broad field of permanent nature like religious education, departments covering special but continuing phases in a division such as leadership training in the field of religious education, and special committees dealing with short-term assignments. The training, when needed, will of course be gauged to the scope and function of the particular group.

In general, training should include a prepared definition or charter of the function to be performed. Such a statement should be terse, yet suitable as a continuing guide to members of the group in their work; this will help to prevent digression from the main objective. A brief statement of the organizational philosophy and objective may be desirable. It should define the extent of responsibility, the relationship to other groups that may be involved, the administrative resources and aids that are available, and other sources of information. Care should be taken to point out the relation of the particular group and its objectives to denominational needs and to those other agencies in the community that may operate in the same field. Policies pertaining to finance, authorization of program, issuance of public statements, and release of publicity should be made clear. Deadlines for reports should be fixed, and the character of reports should be described.

In the case of permanent units, such as divisions or departments working under budget provisions, it is desirable that the board of the unit submit for approval a set of bylaws that govern its procedure. Staff advisers, including the chief executive, should share in such an undertaking before the proposed bylaws are submitted to the board of directors for their approval in conference with the chief executives and the board of directors.

Opportunity should be given for working groups to appear before governing bodies, such as the council assembly and the board of directors, to present plans or report on activities. Suitable recognition and praise of work accomplished are important; formal recognition after the assigned task is completed makes for continuing interest and good public relations.

The executive will be concerned to provide suitable collateral reading for staff and committee personnel. Many parallels may be found in the secular field, or in denominations or councils of churches, state or national. Attention is called to the many excellent books now available on the functions of the executive and the conduct of boards and committees.

In the case of permanent working groups, efforts should be made to secure the attendance of such division and department personnel at conferences and institutes, even though such gatherings may be planned primarily for professional workers. By such methods staff and committee personnel may be made more effective. And it is important to establish training programs.

Chapter 8

PROGRAM BUILDING
· ·

Hugh Chamberlín Burr

The activities that churches decide to carry out together by means of a council depend on several factors. But first we need to note the two basic considerations that apply to all programs—their continuance as well as their initiation. An effective program must have two things: a small group that will give it loving concern, and adequate time for the solution of the problem. This means assigning one project to one committee, and then giving it adequate time to formulate its proposals.

The second consideration is an opportunity to establish this proposed program as a part of the over-all function of a council in terms of strategy, finance, and priority. If it should not be out of line with other ongoing programs, if adequate finance is or can be made available, and if it is something that the representatives of all the interests in a council agree should be done now, the way is clear. Otherwise, of course, unhappiness and ineffectiveness may be the only results of a project initiated without such due regard for over-all strategy, assured financial undergirding, and agreed priority.

History is one of the first of the major factors. In any council's life, that which has gone before modifies the present. Even at the beginning of a council, the steps leading to its formation, and the embryonic organization from which it usually develops, contain experiences of co-operation, some few perhaps unhappy, but most of them happy. The happy ones are naturally stabilized in the current and continuing program; they have become "natural."

Factors Determining Program

At the beginning of the council movement the three concerns that most often led to co-operative action were those for the extension of the kingdom, for civic righteousness, and for Christian education. The eagerness to make an impression on a community by doing together in the area of evangelism what most churches were accustomed to do separately, created a mighty push toward a permanent organization. The value to a council in promoting co-operative evangelism has been demonstrated again and again, and the desirability of united action in evangelism continues as strong as it ever was. In a division of life and work, co-operative evangelism stands out as pre-eminently necessary and possible.

The concern for civic righteousness has likewise continued strong. A department of social righteousness or Christian social relations or Christian social progress is part of the answer to the question easily but unthinkingly asked, "Why doesn't the church do something about" some social evil. "The church," a theological term, is hardly an agent in sociological activity. Even "the churches" in a council may not be, because of their differing conceptions of what is right among differing denominations. The wider the organization fellowship, therefore, the wider may be the areas of disagreement as well as of agreement. The concerns for world peace, good industrial practices, and civic honesty continue in the area of agreement, and point the way to a program. Should a "crusade" become necessary on any of these matters, a separate temporary organization for this one purpose, in which all the members think and feel alike, may be not only the best solution but the only one.

Felt needs are another factor in determining program. Therefore we must look over the programs of other councils, not with the idea of noting "what is done that we don't do," but to discover pertinent areas of service that would meet the needs of our community.

Even when a program, successful elsewhere, is in the process of being adapted by a local council to fit its own situation, the operation of the new program should not be begun until in addition to its acceptance it has met the three standards mentioned above—strategy, finance, and timeliness. In the final analysis local conditions and felt needs are the determining elements in program building.

Another factor that determines program is to be found in those changes in the responsibility of a community that cannot be foreseen. A nearby government installation is an illustration: what ought the churches to do together about it? A frank facing of that problem in which timeliness is not an optional factor may lead to rapid changes in program due to over-all strategy either within the financial resources, or for which financial resources must be found.

Another factor that determines program is to be found in the new features of our everyday life—radio and TV, films and filmstrips. Twenty-five years ago a council with a radio department could scarcely have been found; nowadays they are common because they are necessary. If the Christian community is to make the best use of these mass media, it must do so "together." This is the point that least needs to be labored, because it is most obvious. What is almost as obvious is that adequate resources for Christian education in the field of audio-visual aids are rarely available to single churches or single denominations. But together our united audio-visual libraries can be of service to all.

Another factor that determines program in a particular area of service is the variety of state laws that affect weekday religious education. Since education in the United States is fortunately a local matter within a framework of state educational law, variety at this point is of forty-eight different kinds—forty-nine if the District of Columbia is included. In addition to state educational law, local customs and regulations and rulings as to educational matters make it necessary for each council to determine how it will function in this field.

In addition to these factors there is one over-all question that has a great deal to do with program, namely, whether the community is large enough to undertake co-operation under paid leadership, or whether because of its smallness it is compelled to think of its co-operation in terms of volunteer leadership. The answer to that question will make a great difference. If volunteer leadership is the solution, much can be gained by enlisting the services of volunteers who are retired from gainful occupations, but whose vision and energy and time can make a great contribution to Christianity when correlated through a council of churches.

Program Scope

Various principles will guide our work together at different periods in our co-operative experience. The criterion at the beginning may well be "What can best be done together." That may be followed by "What can only be done together." In both cases the projection is from the individual congregation or denomination to the group. Since the purpose back of all co-operative endeavor is a more widespread service, a more comprehensive influence, a greater impact, a more effective witness, the point of reference should change, so that some day we may be doing together everything that does not need to be done by individual churches.

Therefore program is a fluid thing. It may lead to a dozen departments, committees, commissions in one division; only one or two in others. The National Council's pattern of four divisions compressed to three under the principle of committee integration in Chapter 3, and two general departments increased to four by the addition of pastors and youth, is suggestive. That pattern, however, does suggest how the presently recognized common concerns of the churches may be related to one another, and thus may highlight what they are. It should frankly be recognized that state and local councils may never have many programs in the area of home and foreign missions, and that life and work and Christian education may be the "natural" location for three-quarters of their programs, but every council will be poorer if it does not have some program in the area of Christian missions and services. ("The Principle of Committee Integration," Chapter 3.)

If a local council builds on its past, is concerned chiefly to follow felt needs, to respond to changes in the community, and to make full use in church life of the new media of communication available in our day, its program will be realistic and vital, fluid rather than static, and always enlarging. Those will be its common characteristics. Their expression will be found in a variety of program services and projects, as listed in the next chapter.

To act within the area of agreement, to keep open the avenues to its enlargement, to seek first the kingdom of our God and of his Christ—these are the chart and compass of our voyage—together.

Chapter 9

DEVELOPING PROGRAM AND SERVICES

William D. Powell

Fellowship in a council brings a greater awareness of people's needs and better ideas for successfully meeting them. Programs grow because a single activity taken together is so useful and the results so inspiring that more is desired. As the fellowship warms, the question frequently arises, "Why not do this together also?" Programs often develop from union services, collective action on a moral issue, or from almost any other church response to human needs.

This fellowship together results in the revelation of other needs that the church representatives have been aware of but have never acted on. When this comes out in a discussion, joint action almost inevitably follows. By such a meeting of concerned minds anxious only to spread the message and practice of the Gospel does the Church of Christ reach out into the community. Practicality and utility are two guiding factors which joined with economy and efficiency make joint action a thrilling and useful contribution to the mission of the Church.

To meet a real need a council may begin an activity in a limited way; as a project or a one-time activity with no intention of going further. But this may reveal other unnoticed areas of Christian concern, so that the original program is repeated and out of it stem additional ones. Thus the activity of a temporary committee may grow into a permanent department, with many committees carrying enlarging responsibilities.

Such developments, however, are usually a matter of years of gradual growth. Sometimes they are the product of changes in leadership. The chairman of a committee may see more needs than his predecessor did; or he may change its emphasis or direction and thereby open new fields of service. Even the rephrasing of a committee's title may open its eyes to new vision. Staff also plays its particular part, because of its knowledge of the churches of the community, its vision of community needs, and its skill in leadership. The community itself may sometimes put new demands on the churches, so that in order to meet them the churches join hands and change or divert a current program or service to meet the new need.

The constant attention of the staff and voluntary leadership to helping the churches fulfill their purpose in the community is the best assurance of the growth and development of the programs and services of a council of churches.

Chapter 10

FUNCTIONS OF BOARDS AND COMMITTEES

· ·

William D. Powell

Although the governing body of a council of churches is its assembly, it generally provides a board of directors, to which between assembly meetings it entrusts most of its powers. This board is expected to have oversight of policy, finance, and program, to assure that all functions of the council accord with the will of the member churches as expressed in the contract of procedure—the constitution and bylaws. The board may or may not be subdivided into committees, depending on the size and structural plan of the council.

On the other hand, a committee is usually assigned a limited responsibility, frequently of one function or service, and often is only temporarily established; when its job is done, it is dismissed. Committees report to the board either because they are parts of it or are appointed by it.

The board normally authorizes the responsibility and limits of the committee function, defines its powers of proceeding, and specifies the funds, if any, at its disposal. Committees are a means of sharing responsibility, of getting the benefit of more detailed participation by skilled individuals, and of including more persons in the council's program and service responsibilities.

Steps like the following suggest how the board and committees of a council provide programs and services:

1. The idea for the program or service either originates in or is referred to the board.
2. If approved, it may be assigned to the proper standing committee, or a new committee may be set up to handle it. Such a committee is instructed as to how far it may proceed without reference back to the board for further authority.
3. Assignments of detailed and specific responsibilities are made to members of the committee and/or to the staff that is related to the function.
4. A time schedule is arranged and agreed on, for each step toward the goal.
5. Plans are determined for promoting attendance at the program or use of the service.
6. The cost is estimated and approved, and funds are provided or otherwise assured.
7. When the program is presented or the service rendered, those who ar-

ranged and directed it are present to see for themselves the reaction it meets and the degree in which it accomplishes its purpose.

8. When the committee finishes its work it reports back to the board or through it to the assembly.

Chapter II

DEVELOPING AN AGENDA

Minor C. Miller

The success of any council of churches, board, or committee meeting will depend in large measure on the degree in which a basic purpose or objective is central in the arrangement of its agenda. Here is a basic principle:

If an executive or administrator knows what he wants to accomplish in a particular board or committee meeting, his skill in agenda planning and arrangement will be a determining factor in the accomplishments of the meeting.

Great care should always be used, at the first meeting of any board or committee, to state clearly the purpose of that meeting. This purpose ought to be stated clearly in writing, and each member of the board or committee should receive a copy in advance of the meeting; this is important. Without listing a multitude of details, the following may be suggestive.

Devotional Service

The agenda of every council of churches board or committee should include a brief period of devotion. The nature of the meeting and the occasion will determine the nature of this service. There should be a prayer, appropriately related to the purpose of the meeting. It is desirable to provide for singing and Scripture, with brief interpretation; but as a rule this service should be very brief. It is important, but its importance is not necessarily increased by its length.

Approval of Minutes

If previous meetings have been held of a particular board or committee, it is always in order to include on the agenda for each meeting the reading, consideration, and approval of the minutes of the previous meeting. If these minutes have been mailed to the members of the board or committee, it may be desirable to consider them without reading them. Decisions on this point should be made by the group.

Use of Factual Material

Every important board or committee ought to receive an abundance of accurate factual information before starting its work. This factual information may come to the board or committee in various ways, but especially in reports from standing or special committees; and such reports ought to appear early on the agenda of board or committee meetings. Here is an illustration:

A. State Council Executive Committee:

Accurate information concerning the operation of the total program of a state council of churches should be presented periodically to its executive committee. This information should come to the executive committee through a series of staff, departmental, and committee reports. Among specific agenda items may be the following:

1. Report of the executive secretary. This should be a general report of the total work of the council.
2. Report of the treasurer.
3. Department reports. Specific information should be given of every aspect of the council's work since the previous report. The agenda should include every department.
4. Miscellaneous reports. These will be made by regular and special committees.

B. Finance Committee of County or City Council of Churches:

In this illustration, it is assumed that the finance committee has met to review the progress that has been made in raising the annual budget. For example, a meeting was held three days after the effort was started. The particular plan of organization will determine the nature of the agenda. In many sitautions, the agenda may call for specific and detailed reports, as follows:

1. Consideration of department problems, including specific recommendations.
2. Financial problems; the development of plans, etc.
3. Staff problems and recommendations.
4. Miscellaneous program items.

C. Suggested Agenda for Executive Committee Meeting:
1. Prayer
2. Introductory statement by the chairman
3. Report of the commission on finance—
   a. Report of the chairman
   b. Report of the treasurer
   c. Report of the auditor
4. Report of the executive secretary
5. Department reports—
   a. Christian education
   b. Christian social relations
   c. Church women

    d. Evangelism and missions

    e. Public relations

    f. Rural church

    g. Youth council

6. Department recommendations for next year (to be presented to the annual meeting)

    a. Christian education

    b. Christian social relations

    c. Church women

    d. Evangelism and missions

    e. Public relations

    f. Rural church

    g. Youth council

7. The budget for next year

8. Amendments to the constitution (to be presented to the annual meeting)

9. Miscellaneous business

10. Adjournment

Chapter 12

PLANNING THE ANNUAL MEETING

. . . .

Minor C. Miller

To prepare a successful annual meeting of a state, county, or city council of churches, all responsible council executives must keep in mind this basic principle:

To promote co-operative church activities, we must expect to exert ten times the effort in order to achieve one-tenth of the reasonable results.

The Call for the Meeting

Those who have the responsibility of directing the preparations for the annual meeting of a state, county, or city council of churches will do well to consider the following:

Fixed Date. In the light of local conditions and after careful study, a council of churches should determine the best time of the year for holding its annual meeting. It may decide, for example, to hold it each year on the first Thursday in January, or on the second Tuesday in July—the particular date is not important; it should be the date agreed on as the best for those who are expected to attend. After this date has been determined, it should be announced from time to time in appropriate council publications.

The First Official Notice. It is suggested that the first official notice of the date should be mailed to all members of the organization at least sixty days beforehand. In this first official notice each member should be asked to send, on the enclosed postcard, a prompt reply indicating whether the member will plan to attend.

Follow-up Notices. Approximately ten days after the first official notice, follow-up letters should be sent. (1) A letter of thanks should be sent to all who indicated that they expect to attend. It will be helpful if this letter can carry some interesting or significant information about the work of the council. (2) A reminder letter should be sent to all members who did not reply to the first official notice. This first reminder letter may properly carry some encouraging news about the development of council work in the state or county or city.

The Second Official Notice. Approximately three weeks before the meeting, a second general letter should be sent to all members. This letter should repeat the date of the meeting, and should tell something of the nature of the business to be considered. It should stress the idea that the attendance of every council member is needed. Special notations should be made in this letter as follows: (1) To those who are coming: "We look forward eagerly to having you present at the annual meeting," etc. (2) To those who have not replied: "You apparently have overlooked my previous letter; there is prospect of a large attendance. We are very anxious to have you meet with us. May I hear from you by next Tuesday?" etc. (3) To those who cannot come: Express regret; if there are alternate members, be sure to arrange for your alternate member to attend, etc.

The Final Notice. This final notice should reach each member two or three days before the meeting. This notice should include some encouraging word of progress in the development of co-operative church work in the area during the past year. But don't tell them too much—aim to "whet their appetites." Assure the members that the cause of co-operative Christianity needs *them* in the approaching annual meeting.

Using the Telephone. If the annual meeting is for a county or city council of churches, plan to have someone call all members the day before or on the morning of the day on which the meeting is to begin. Simply say, "We are calling in the interest of the annual meeting. We are glad you are coming," or "We shall surely miss you."

The Purpose of the Annual Meeting

The success of an annual meeting will always be measured by the extent to which it aids in clarifying and forwarding the purpose of the organization; every annual meeting should be planned to accomplish this clarifying and forwarding. When you are planning *any* type of council meeting, ask yourself this basic question: "What is the purpose of the organization I have been called to serve?" Write down your best answers, and then ask yourself these further questions: "What phases of our council work seem to be making good and substantial progress?" "Is it probable that all council members have a clear and adequate understanding of why they have been called to serve as members of the local council?" When you have answered these questions, you may be ready to turn your approaching annual meeting into an instrument of very great opportunity.

The Purpose Illustrated

Here are some illustrations of purpose.

A council executive became convinced that the churches in his area were in great need of more leadership education. He had been working with the state denominational executives, but progress had been slow. These denominational executives had been friendly to the council, but they had never quite seen how they could use the facilities of the state council to help solve their common leadership education problems. After many conferences and several years of effort, the state council executive thought of using its approaching annual meeting as an opportunity to forward that phase of work so greatly needed. He engaged the service of a leader from the national office of one of the denominations of his state—a man known to be friendly toward the National Council of Churches and toward its leadership education curriculum. This outstanding

75

leader came to the state council annual meeting, and explained in some detail how his and other denominations had developed plans for co-operative leadership education in local communities. The members of the local councils were amazed at the progress that national denominational boards had made in co-operative leadership education over a third of a century. "Co-operative leadership education is practical for scores of communities in the state," the visiting speaker said. Numbers of council members asked many questions, which this visiting leader helped to answer. His message and his illustrations so inspired this annual meeting that it appointed a committee to work with all the denominational executives in the state, and to bring back a comprehensive plan of leadership education for the whole state.

In one city council, each successive annual meeting had emphasized the lack of funds. There had been occasional deficits, and the distressing financial situation was embarrassing to everyone, but no one did anything about it. One year, however, the situation changed. The preceding annual meeting had appointed a prominent layman as chairman of the finance committee. At his suggestion, the executive committee then elected seven equally prominent men and women from seven other denominations. This group met monthly for a whole year. They got information as to how councils of churches were financed in other states. As the next annual meeting approached, it was decided that the meeting should consider ways and means for securing adequate funds for co-operative church work in that city. When the finance committee submitted its report, three of the most prominent ministers followed (they had previously been asked to speak). Questions were asked and answered, and all the council members obviously approved the report of the finance committee. After thorough discussion, the meeting voted to request all co-operating churches to secure for co-operative church work in the city and state a minimum of 1.5 per cent of the local expense budget of the co-operating churches. This successful annual meeting thus did something good for every phase of co-operative church work in that city.

Reviewing Activities

A successful annual meeting will devote adequate time to review all the council activities of the previous year. Those who are responsible for planning an annual meeting will surely plan to use various visual means and devices for presenting these activities clearly and concisely—maps, charts, slides, and so on. The annual meeting should receive a written report of every council department or committee, and these reports should become a part of the recorded minutes of the organization.

Maps and charts and graphs should be used wherever and whenever these devices will help to present an accurate picture of the work of the council during the previous year. These illustrative devices should not only show its accomplishments, but they should also emphasize the areas of need and of opportunity for co-operative Christianity in the state, county, or city. Council executives should use their opportunity to tell the whole story accurately, concisely, and movingly. The manner in which the record of achievement is presented to the annual meeting will have an important effect on the success of the entire program of the council.

Relate the Annual Meeting to Basic Principles

A successful annual meeting will give very careful consideration to all those activities that appear to be needed and practical, from the point of view of the basic purpose of the organization.

What can a council of churches do? It can do anything its members agree to do. How is it possible to discover what council members *want to do* in a particular area? By means of guided discussion in a council annual meeting, it should be possible to determine the general area of activity that council members want to cultivate co-operatively. In beginning such discussions, we must consider these basic principles:

Common Needs. It has been well said that every person is born with a positive religious nature, and is endowed with the capacity to live a religious life. As an ancient writer said, "God created man in his own image . . . and breathed into his nostrils the breath of life; and man became a living being" (Gen. 1:27, 2:7). With due allowance for differences of opinion, Christians generally have been sympathetic with this point of view. The human race has possibilities for spiritual development. The church is dedicated to the task of helping individual persons to grow more nearly into the stature of the fullness of Jesus Christ.

As we apply these facts to the developing program of co-operative Christianity, we see that the churches recognize that every person needs spiritual guidance. Those who have never come under the influence of the Christian Gospel are in need of evangelism. Those who have pledged their faith in Christ are always in need of Christian nurture. The churches recognize that this need for spiritual growth is universal. The recognition of this need is a basic principle of co-operative church work. And the annual meeting affords a good opportunity for council leaders to discuss the principle.

Common Faith. The churches share a common faith, which is rooted in the Bible. The Bible is used and treasured by all Christian denominations. Co-operative church work is more possible because of the unity of the faith that is centered in the Bible.

If anyone should doubt that Protestant Christians share a common faith, he should enter on a period of experimentation. It is very revealing to discover what intelligent Christians of different denominations actually believe about God, about Jesus and his teachings, or about prayer, immortality, and other phases of Christian truth. One can start such an investigation by making inquiry of friends in three or four denominations regarding what they believe about prayer or other aspects of Christian faith. This type of investigation always makes it clear that Christians do share a common faith. It would be well to take a look at this principle in the council's annual meeting.

Common Responsibility. Every Christian shares with every other Christian

77

a certain responsibility for the religious conditions in this community. In view of the fact that Christians in the community are members of different denominations, it follows that the churches are jointly responsible for supplying the unmet religious needs of the community. The degree in which each church is able to sense this common community responsibility will determine the nature and extent of the program of co-operative church work in the community.

There is always need for evangelism and nurture. Secular thought and practices still dominate the life of many communities. Increasingly the churches are recognizing their joint responsibility, but there is need for a great co-operative advance. Indeed, the religious and moral tone of a community can probably not be permanently improved without the joint effort of its churches. The participation of a great many people in the discussion of this principle will contribute to the success of an annual meeting.

Common Plans and Procedures. The effective promotion of co-operative church work will depend on the development of common plans and procedures. Before a group of churches can work effectively in their community, they will need to develop a common and effective agency through which they can work. A successful program of co-operative church work will always depend on an effective plan of interchurch organization in the community.

Through long experience in almost every section of the United States, the place and value of county and city councils of churches has been clearly demonstrated. These organizations are essential and necessary in any plan for advancing the cause of co-operative Christianity. The time has come when ministers and laymen (men, women, and young people) should have regular and frequent opportunity to counsel together regarding the status and influence of Christianity in their community. Don't forget to use the annual meeting as a time when council members can have a share in determining the nature of the co-operative program for their committee or state.

Present Specific Proposals

After council members have arrived at a fairly accurate understanding of basic principles and policies, it is highly appropriate that the council's several departments or its regular or special committees recommend to the annual meeting specific items for consideration and action. For example, if the council's department of evangelism or of Christian social relations should desire to propose that the council undertake or expand a co-operative ministry to agricultural migrants, the particular department should present to the annual meeting specific facts about the need, the proposed plan of operation, and its estimated costs. Through discussion, the members of the council at the annual meeting will be able to determine whether they desire to enlarge or improve this particular project.

In one city the council's department of Christian education had from time to time given casual consideration to weekday religious education. But they had never done anything but talk! Finally talk was turned into action, after the council's department of Christian education had submitted to the council's annual meeting numerous facts about weekday religious education. A discussion followed. The members of the council were definitely interested. The committee was continued and enlarged. After the adjournment several members said, "Didn't we have a good meeting? It looks as though we are going to get somewhere now."

Summary

In considering this subject of how to plan a successful annual meeting we have emphasized the following:

1. Be very careful and very persistent about the *call* for the meeting.
2. Relate every annual meeting as closely as possible to the purpose of the council.
3. Provide for accurate review and clear illustrations of the activities of the council during the previous year.
4. Use the annual meeting to help clarify well defined principles.
5. The council's departments and committees should present specific proposals as clearly and convincingly as possible.

Chapter 13

RELATIONSHIPS

John W. Harms

Local councils of churches have an intricate set of relationships with their member local churches and the denominational organizations of these churches. State councils have equally intricate relations with their constituent denominational units, and in some cases with units of constituent local councils of churches. Councils also have to maintain relationships with a complicated network on the community level with community agencies, and on the state level with various state agencies.

The basic pattern of these relationships is set by the inherent nature of a council of churches, which has already been considered (see Chapters 2 and 3). Above all, councils are an expression of the corporate life and aspirations of the churches. They are "interchurch" (or interdenominational) organizations; not non- or extra-church (or nondenominational).

Councils are growing institutions, not only in size and outreach but in their basic purposes, structure, and program. Although a rich and valuable ecumenical tradition has developed that should be better analyzed and interpreted than it has been, it is still too early to make a definitive statement about the life and work of councils. But certain basic considerations appear so clear that they ought to be stated as characteristic of the council movement in its present stage of development.

Relationships to Denominations

A local council of churches composed of local congregations is the agency of the denominations at work in the local community. But the starting point for the consideration of a council's relationship to its local member churches is the denominations of which the member churches are units. The denominations are the most powerful influences that shape the life and work of the local churches, and therefore of local councils.

These denominations may vary in their attitudes toward state and local councils of churches. But their membership in world and national ecumenical organizations inevitably carries with it a commitment to the ecumenical principle as an active principle in the local community. The World Council's message to the churches issued at Amsterdam in 1948 said:

" . . . Here at Amsterdam we have committed ourselves afresh to Him, and

80

have covenanted with one another in constituting this World Council of Churches. We intend to stay together. We call upon Christian congregations everywhere to endorse and fulfill this covenant in their relations one with another."

This was reiterated at Evanston. The message to the churches issued at Evanston in 1954 stated:

"Now we would speak through our member churches directly to each congregation. Six years ago our churches entered into a covenant to form this Council, and affirmed their intention to stay together. We thank God for his blessing on our work and fellowship during these six years. We enter now upon a second stage. To stay together is not enough. We must go forward. As we learn more of our unity in Christ, it becomes the more intolerable that we should be divided. We therefore ask you: Is your church seriously considering its relation to other churches in the light of our Lord's prayer that we may be sanctified in the truth and that we may all be one? Is your congregation, in fellowship with sister congregations around you, doing all it can do to ensure that your neighbors shall hear the voice of the one Shepherd calling all men into the one flock?"

The constituent denominations of the National Council of the Churches of Christ in the U.S.A. have recognized that local community interchurch co-operation is essential. Through its General Board the National Council has made the following declaration:

"At the biennial meeting of the National Council of Churches at Denver a penetrating remark of a seminary student was reported. After a day and a half of the experience of that gathering, which demonstrated the degree to which we have discovered our oneness in Christ, he said, 'This is wonderful here, but there is something wrong because this spirit is not present in the local community where I live.'

"If the churches are to be together in a spirit of oneness, that spirit must be manifest in the local community, where the people who compose the churches come into the most intimate touch with each other. It is there the members of various congregations intermingle. If co-operative Christianity has been beneficial at the national level, how much more valuable would be a spirit of oneness or wholeness in the body of Christians in a local community.

"At Denver it was said: 'The Christian witness is one witness. It is the testimony of persons who have participated in the joyous experience set forth in the Gospel. It brings to bear upon a secular society the impact of the Christian community. This is one task.' However, this 'Christian community' in a local situation ought to be united in spirit and co-ordinated in action.

"The leadership of the churches which constitute the National Council must accept the responsibility of encouraging this spirit at local levels. It is inconsistent to place a local congregation in a position of conflicting loyalties if it recognizes its denominational relationship and also desires to take its rightful part in the Christian fellowship in its community. The way to avoid this ought not to be too difficult if we set our minds to it.

"The goal will be achieved only by the active effort of the denominational leaders of the churches of the National Council. Local congregations will be guided by their respective denominations.

"Thirty communions have banded together in the National Council of Churches in a common task. We cannot truly say the churches are together, however, until we mean that the people who compose the churches and who live in local communities have also become aware of their oneness in Christ. To help bring about such awareness is a pressing task of the National Council."*

Relationships to Local Churches

The relationships of local councils to local churches grow out of the relationship of local churches to one another. When local councils are properly constituted they are created and maintained by the official action of local congregations.

These joint actions of local churches may be described as:

1. A "covenant," which is what the communions of the World Council of Churches have declared their relationship with each other to be. "We . . . have covenanted with one another in constituting the World Council of Churches."

2. Local councils may be described as a partnership that has been established among local churches so that they may accomplish certain aspects of their common mission. The analogy of a business partnership applies at least in part. The partnership consists of congregations that are parts of sovereign and independent denominations, which nevertheless recognize a spiritual and a structural relationship with each other. This partnership has been created for specifically recognized purposes, which are to be implemented in ways to be agreed on among the "partners" (congregations) as the "partnership" (council) moves forward from year to year.

The purposes of this partnership (council) have already been stated (see Chapters 3, 10, and 11). Generally speaking they will be found at three points: on the community level, where the churches must "aggregate" their resources of leadership, money, and skill if they are to be effective; in collective self-service activities for purposes of economy or effectiveness; and for the spiritual fellowship that they have together through a common loyalty to Jesus Christ as the divine revelation of God.

3. The council relationship may be thought of not only as a covenant and a partnership, but also as joint boards of strategy for the churches of a community. In the smaller communities, especially, the combined official boards of the member churches might constitute the council, which in effect would be a community-wide "Joint Official Board" of the churches. Some experimenting is being done with this idea. We must realize that an effective council basically depends on an intelligent and enthusiastic commitment to the ecu-

---

* Statement on: "Strengthening Co-operation in States and Local Communities," adopted by the General Board, National Council of Churches, May 19, 1953.

menical ideal in each member congregation, and on an understanding of the corporate mission of the churches to community life.

Relationship to the Community and Its Agencies

"Let the church be the church" was one of the great statements that issued from the Oxford Conference on Life and Work in 1937. Properly understood, this may well be the watchword of councils of churches. But just how to work this principle into actual practice is at times a baffling problem. In the everyday practice of community life, what should be the relationships of the churches and their councils to the community and its agencies?

Community responsibilities rest squarely on the churches, and cannot be shifted to councils of churches. The councils are instruments through which the social mission of the churches may be accomplished. This is fundamental in council-local church relationships.

Another basic consideration is that the churches should not undertake to dominate the organizational life of the community. Councils often—especially in the first enthusiastic flush of their existence—yield to the temptation to "throw their weight around," and thus give an impression that the churches' function is to dictate the moral, political, and civic life of the community. But in spirit if not in fact this attitude violates the basic principle of the separation of church and state. It is authoritarian if not totalitarian in spirit, and therefore is a denial of freedom. Therefore both Protestant laymen and ministers reject such leadership by the churches. It is contrary to the fundamental teachings of the churches, which are committed to freedom as a primary quality of social organization and human relationships.

The principle of the separation of church and state gives the churches a very significant and creative relationship to the community. The principles involved have not perhaps been well enough clarified, but some clearly defined practices may be seen in the most successful experience of the councils in the last thirty years. This experience shows that the churches themselves, individually and collectively, must create the climate and leadership for sound community relationships through councils of churches. This calls for such individual and collective action as the following:

1. The churches' function is to teach both the general principles of citizenship and their specific application to contemporary community life. This and other functions to be named depend on the councils having sound factual data properly interpreted. In states and larger cities this means an adequate research staff, but it is no less essential in smaller communities, where adequate information may be secured by volunteer workers.

2. The churches should inspire and enlist their members for specific leadership and service functions in the community and its agencies.

3. The churches should encourage the formation of citizens' organizations where men and women of all faiths may join in common efforts for community betterment.

4. The churches should at the proper times undertake to mediate the

83

judgment and love of God to community life, as important issues arise where distinctly moral and spiritual values are at stake. When this function is undertaken in a spirit of humility and repentance as well as forgiveness it is usually recognized as a proper function of the churches.

One way to summarize is to describe a council of churches as the nexus between the individual churches and the corporate life of the community. The churches provide the ideals and create the convictions, the leadership, and the will to realize Christian goals in community life. The councils co-ordinate and unify these efforts, and thus bring them to focus on the common life of the community through their own efforts, but also through volunteer civic organizations and through official municipal agencies.

Council executives know that baffling problems often arise about council membership in community organizations, and sometimes questions arise about its holding membership in community agencies. But in view of the considerations stated above, councils as official representatives of the churches must participate in community organizations that carry forward the ideals and purposes held by the churches—provided they bear in mind the following principles:

1. There should be an understanding among the churches of the policy that is being followed.

2. The council should be related only to those community organizations whose objectives and methods conform in principle and practice to those of the churches as these are authorized by the council.

3. There should be responsible participation by official representatives of the council in organizations in which the council holds membership. Unless this can take place the council should not participate or allow its name to be used as a front.

4. When emergencies call for action, the proper officers and executives should be given enough freedom to function as responsible Christian leaders.

Relationships to State Councils of Churches

Local councils are usually member units of the state councils of churches. There are variations in practice among the state councils, but this would be considered as normal procedure (see Chapter 5).

In states where there are strong city councils there have sometimes been tensions between them and the state organizations. There are unresolved problems in local-state council relationships to which everyone concerned should give careful and patient attention.

Local, city, and county councils must realize that there is great need for strong state councils of churches. There is as much need for a state-wide strategy for protestantism as there is for a local community strategy. Local councils should therefore participate and be prepared to give leadership to state council work. Local councils without specialized professional leadership must depend on the state councils for much of the professional leadership they need. State councils in turn must be prepared to give such leadership to local councils. Even strong, well led city councils need that leadership and service that only strong state councils can provide. And if perchance they do not themselves feel that need, they still have an obligation to share generously in the development of the ecumenical movement in less well developed communities.

Relationship to the National Council of the Churches of Christ in the U.S.A.

Local councils are related to the National Council indirectly through their state councils. There is much discussion among council people about this relationship, and there is the hope that a more satisfactory relationship may be worked out whereby local, county, city, and state ecumenical organizations may be more adequately represented in the national organization.

At present the Constitution of the National Council provides, in Article IV, Section 3, that "The co-operative work of the churches in the various states, cities, and counties shall have representation in the General Assembly in the following manner:

"For states—[Article IV, Section 3 a] One representative for each state council of churches which, by action of its highest constitutional authority, has declared itself in agreement with the Preamble of this Constitution and which has been constituted by the communions in its area." (The Preamble reads: "In the Providence of God, the time has come when it seems fitting more fully to manifest oneness in Jesus Christ as Divine Lord and Savior.")

"For cities and counties—[Article IV, Section 3 b] Ten additional representatives, at least three of whom shall be women, elected by the General Board from nominations by the city and county councils, each of which, by action of its highest constitutional authority, has declared itself in agreement with the Preamble of this Constitution and which is constituted by the communions in its area."

The Constitution further provides that "Each such representative shall be a member in good and regular standing of a communion included in the membership of the Council, or of a communion which in the judgment of the General Board is eligible for membership, and shall serve only when approved by action of his communion. Whenever voting in the General Assembly is by communions, these representatives shall vote with the communions of which they are members."

In Article IX, Section 3 c, which deals with membership on the General Board, Subsection c provides that "The representatives of the co-operative work of the churches in state and local councils of churches appointed to the General Assembly as authorized in Article IV, Section 3, of this Constitution shall name to the General Board one-seventh of the number of their representatives, but not less than five, of whom one-third, or not less than two, shall be women."

In matters of program local councils have an obligation to implement in the

85

local community the co-operative programs of the denominations that are developed through the divisions and departments of the National Council. Some progress is being made in the matter of co-ordinated denominational program emphases, so that when the ongoing programs of the denominations reach their local churches they, in turn, can work unitedly in the community. This begins to appear as a realizable goal, though it may yet take many years to achieve in full.

The many valuable program resources available to local councils from the National Council are stated in another section (see Chapter 17).

Relationships to Councils of Church Men and Church Women, Ministers' Associations, and Youth Councils

In Chapter 3 "The Principle of Inclusiveness" is given as one of the foundation principles of all councils of churches. "Protestant-Orthodox Christianity achieves a greater functional solidarity and effectiveness where it is possible for it to work together through one inclusive organization." This is the ideal that this principle stresses. Within this pattern councils of church women and church men, ministers' associations, and youth councils may be general departments of councils of churches if mutually agreed on (See Chapter 5, "Suggested Constitutions"). This would permit the real integration of the total co-operative program. Circumstances, historical and contemporary, may sometimes not permit the immediate achievement of this ideal. Where this is true, sharing equitably in the administration of common activities to attain common ends, and working together, are the best approaches for securing the fuller program and organization integration that is our ideal.

Since one inclusive organization is the goal toward which we all wish to work, the following procedures may be helpful.

1. When any one of these organizations becomes a general department and is made up of responsible and approved representatives of the churches, it should have autonomy, consistent with the general principles of the council, in its determination of its officers, program, budget, and financial operation.

2. When, by mutual agreement, the budgets of general departments are included in the regular budget of the council, all members of the council family will have an equal concern for the financial success of the council's total program. The methods of raising the various budgets, and the allocation of responsibility for income and operating expenses, should be reached after consultation and agreement of all concerned.

3. The program will be enriched and made more effective when it is developed co-operatively, so as to avoid parallelism or duplication.

Addenda

Suggested criteria for the organizational participation of councils of church women in state and local councils of churches, as adopted by the General Department of United Church Women:

1. Organizational integration should be adopted only as a result of the objective consideration of the state and local situation, the study of possible patterns of co-operation, and mutual agreement among all interested groups.

2. It should provide for a more adequate participation of the council of church women in policy building, by the inclusion of officers and committee chairmen on the board of directors, and on the executive, nominating, and program committees of the council of churches, and by the inclusion of voting delegates from the council of church women to the annual meeting of the council of churches.

3. It should provide for autonomy in the operation of distinctly United Church Women programs and projects.

4. It should assure the control by the council of church women of their financial operations in such things as budget and bank accounts, council of church women signatures on council of church women checks, the protection of designated funds, and should provide by mutual agreement for the allocation of responsibility for operating expenses.

5. The council of church women treasurer or finance chairman, and preferably one or two other representatives (in the larger councils) should serve on the finance, budget, and/or business committees of the council of churches.

6. In order to enable church women to participate more fully in the annual meeting of the council of churches, it may be desirable to hold the annual meeting of the council of church women at a different time.

Chapter 14

ADMINISTRATIVE PRINCIPLES AND PROCEDURES
. . . .

Forrest C. Weir

Administration in the life of any organization involves many separate but converging lines of action. In this chapter attention is focused on the point of convergence, because that is the center of direction for the life of the organization. Thus, administration may be defined as the system of relationships and procedures that enable the organization to accomplish its declared purpose.

The Nature of Administrative Responsibility

If the carefully wrought pattern described in the constitution and bylaws of a council of churches is taken seriously, the object it sets forth must be regarded as the primary aim of its administrative action. If the representative principle means anything, it locates the initiative and activity in the constituent communions. It is the processes of representation that draw them together into group action. This group action constitutes the general frame within which the administration of the council must work. Its duty, then, is to take these group plans, purposes, and policies, and give them reality.

Strictly speaking, administration is concerned only with the proper working of the instrument set up to accomplish the objectives of the organization. In a council of churches, however, administrative leadership must do much more. All parts of the council must be made conscious of its general mission in the community. The component parts have to understand each other. Beyond this, the working relationships that actually constitute the machinery of operation must be made real. Thus the lubricant of a common mind must be achieved by a variety of procedures designed to allow the different individuals and groups, working together, to achieve the feeling of common responsibility—the feeling of belonging together.

This common mind must then be given direction, so there is an awareness of the general aims toward which all the component parts are laced together into one conscious and coherent whole. Comfortable working relationships, a clear sense of direction, even an awareness of wholeness, important as they are, are not sufficient to make an organization successful. The intangible quality that provides dynamic movement or inspiration must be added. All this a wise and balanced administrative leadership must undertake.

The Nature of Council Organization

The whole structure of a council is comprised of a large number of voluntary contributors. These are of many different types—those who provide material resources, those who provide leadership, those who share in the deliberative processes of assemblies, those who give effect to decisions and judgments. All these, and the churches from which they come, will show a wide and colorful variety. Among them there surely is potential conflict. But this variety must be brought into co-operation, and this latent conflict into a warm solidarity, out of which comes a fellowship of rich texture and great strength.

This system of contributors falls into three groups. First are the churches, which range in thought and forms of work and worship from one end of a scale to the other. Their relationship to each other will show congeniality, indifference, or conflict. They have to be seen also in the context of their community, which in turn consists of a visible complex of activities, organizations, and influences. Second, there is the organization itself, with a variety of participants— the assembly, the officers, the board of directors, and the chairmen and members of committees, constituting "the council." These elements of the council's life will reflect both the common feeling and the points of tension in the churches and the community from which they are drawn. Third, there is the cluster of persons and operations concerned in the ongoing work of the council, the board of directors, the executive staff, and the clerical and maintenance personnel.

These levels overlap; yet to understand their relationships properly, administration must at times separate each from the others, and view each in its immediate environment. The primary concern will more often be to achieve a synthesis of understanding, action, and devotion that can give form, direction, and vitality to the whole program of the council. It will strive to see that each of these different parts not only understands its relationships to the others, but also the direction in which the whole program is moving. Administration will need to make the council see beyond the variety and unity it exhibits in its own life to its share in the same type of fellowship at the national and world levels.

Communication

Basic to all other procedures in administrative leadership is an adequate system of communication that successfully conveys both information and interpretation. This system of communication has to point in two directions. It must inform the churches about the community in which they live, of the actions, decisions, and actual program developed by the co-operative agency as such. For, as the council operates in the community, its many units will draw together a body of practical experience that can give new dimensions to the insights and the vision of each member church. This added dimension is essential to the spirited participation of the church or communion in the total work of its own co-operative agency.

Communication, as it is most commonly thought of in connection with administration, is, however, pointed in the opposite direction. It works through the legislative processes of the organization to the points of execution. This would involve plans, for example, being developed by the board of directors, committed to the charge of administration at its highest level, and then disseminated through the departments for definite action. This envisages a system of connections by which policies beginning at a definite point may proceed outward to enlarging circles of action. That organization is most efficient that can reduce these points of transmission to the smallest number needed to reach all its parts. The number of these points of transmission depends on the size of the organization, but rarely will any council of churches be large enough to need more than three levels of communication—from the legislative body, either the assembly or the board of directors, to the general executive; from the general executive to division or department heads; and from them to the subcommittee or departmental staff members.

This line of communication should be concerned with far more than simply transmitting official decisions and agreements. It must also carry an adequate interpretation of the churches, of their relationship to the community, and an awareness of the coercive factors surrounding the decisions made by the organs of the official life that these churches have instituted. Likewise, it should carry adequate interpretation of the larger sphere of action within which each member works, so that division and department heads and leaders of subunits in the council have a sense of their contribution to an inclusive whole.

Motivation

Effective communication depends as much on the voluntary response of the many contributors as on skill in desseminating information. The decisive investment of devotion that means the difference between mediocrity and inspired performance cannot be commanded. It must be elicited. The question of motivation applies more particularly to those engaged full-time in the work of the council; but it does not exclude the voluntary contributors who participate as chairmen or committee or board members. Anyone carrying any degree of responsibility anywhere in the organization needs to feel strongly spontaneous compulsions to make his response with vigor and constancy.

Administration has a primary duty at the point of incentives. At the lowest level it has to understand and so arrange the material rewards that the participants do not feel that they are being used or exploited, but that everything is being done to give material compensation at a reasonable level for the efforts they are making. Everyone recognizes, however, that material rewards are not fully adequate. Administration has to move on, and guide the relationships of workers in the council into a satisfactory fellowship. Personnel management covers the relations of one individual to another, as well as the relation of the individual to his job.

But there is still a higher level, where the most enduring incentives are awakened. Perhaps it rests on happy personal relationships and individual job adjustment, but it embraces much more. Everyone must feel that he and his efforts constitute an essential part in the working of the whole organization.

90

Thus, the morale that permeates the whole will come to enliven the insights and inspire the action of each individual. This factor is indispensable to effective work, for it overcomes the lassitude that results from indirection or a sense of scattered and dispersed efforts. It cannot be cultivated directly, but springs concomitantly from an appreciation of the vital significance of the enterprise of which one is a part. In a council the seat of such an appreciation is in the persuasive and winsome communication of the spiritual mission of the entire ecumenical movement. This becomes important when a council undertakes diversified services that require the clustering into separately organized departments of expert personnel, many of whom have been drawn to the position they occupy not so much because of any comprehension or skill in co-operative relationships as because of their competence in their specialized fields.

It is the duty of administration to bring all specialized fields—indeed all divisions, departments, and subunits of the council—to discover this larger perspective. When this is done, participation in the work of the organization is not primarily for the maintenance of the organization itself, but for the accomplishment of the larger goal to which it in turn is devoted. This sense of movement with a compelling idea for the future at length creates an enduring sense of unity. And unity in a council of churches is essential if it is to cultivate the conditions that will work for a more permanent and enduring unity among the churches themselves.

The procedures that will develop such motivation among all who are responsible for the life and work of a council must provide for three distinct processes of common experience. One is at the point of planning. Each worker must have a creative role in determining what is to be done. This will at once give him the opportunity to share the best that is in him, and at the same time to receive the best from his fellow workers. The give and take of discussion and group action is the very stuff of group solidarity, for it enables workers to achieve identification with the central purposes of the organization itself. The second is at the level of devotion. Thus, recurrent experiences of worship together, as workers in the same common field, provide the opportunity for lasting spiritual sanctions on the undertaking in which all are engaged, and at the same time the opportunity of self-commitment through the tasks at hand. The third requires occasions large enough and vital enough to unite the whole complex of contributors—delegates, board members, commission and committee members, chairmen, officers, staff—in a keenly satisfying fellowship. This might be a retreat or a banquet, but it should include only those who are to some degree committed to participation in the council.

Ambiguities

In any voluntary organization, where divisions of labor and responsibility have to be arrived at by consent and agreement, a certain amount of overlapping among individuals and groups is bound to occur. Yet without enough clearly recognized integration to insure purposive movement, the organization flounders. This situation is acute in a council of churches, where the double op-

91

portunity of misunderstanding or friction arises from the—as yet—occasional nature of interdenominational contacts, and from the uncertainty within the council set-up as to where and between whom the functions should be divided. This is difficult enough at the point of program and activities. But if there is too much overlapping, or even a high degree of uncertainty as to the lines of responsibility for each unit in the structure of the council, the result is enervating frustration.

Although the interlacing lines of responsibility are held together by voluntary sanctions, they are in no sense capricious. They are definite and responsible commitments, resting on the integrity of a covenant. And this writer believes implicitly that finally they rest on the express will of God. Actual weakness in any unit—say, the board of directors, a department, or executive staff—will certainly affect the operation at all levels. But weakness that can be tagged at any given point usually indicates a chain of weakness which runs through several points. A weak board of directors reflects an indifferent assembly; casual actions of an assembly reflect indifference in the constituent churches.

Administration must work constantly at the elimination of ambiguities that result from poorly delineated responsibilities. Everyone in a staff ought to have a reliable and objective definition of his duties. This principle applies to the structural organs of the council. Neither the individuals nor the divisions of a council can be held responsible for matters over which they have no control. Thus initiative, authority, and responsibility go hand in hand. The churches must have an understanding of their duty in order to make the representative process work through the assembly.

To that end constant reports should go to the churches. The board of directors must know at least within general bounds what its mandate is, on which it must give annual account to the assembly. The general executive, though necessarily required to adjust to a fluid situation, must know definitely his authority, and therefore his responsibility. Of this he must report to the board. Departmental heads will in a similar way receive from and report to the executive and the board.

Our constitutions and bylaws have in the past been very indefinite on these points. The general executive, for example, has often been charged under a constitutional directive that states with inclusive and grand promise: ". . . he shall be responsible for the conduct of the affairs of the Council, subject to the Board of Directors." Then other sections proceed to say that "the Board shall organize and supervise" practically every operative procedure, from program analysis to the employment of clerical personnel, though no clarification is given as to how a deliberative body can act on administrative involvements. The only thing that saves such a situation is the good judgment by which both staff and board transcend its inherent ambiguities.

There is no reason why the bylaws of a council of churches should not clearly define the general area of responsibility that belongs uniquely to the board of directors, so it has complete freedom not only to formulate but also to supervise the carrying out of the general policies and the program objectives, and to appraise and direct the community relationships a council of churches must embrace. Nor is there any reason why the board should not assign without equivocation a similar area of duty to the general executive, so that he may order the day-to-day procedures, decisions, and plans, through which the rigidities of organization may be overcome and vitality and growth achieved, and at the same time hold the power of judgment on the executive in the hands of the board and finally in the assembly.

The Role of Leadership

So far we have been discussing administration as a process that involves many component parts, but our discussion has led naturally to the point where we realize that its effective working is dependent on the role of leadership. The adequate awareness of objectives, a complete and workable system of the relationships of component groups and individuals, the integration of effort, vital interpretations, and the necessary spark of initiative—all these require a point of unity around which all these elements converge. Only as the general executive supplies this imaginative leadership can the synthesis of planning, of reporting, of expanding actions, and of measuring results be brought into one whole and effective pattern. Some attention must therefore be given to the role of the administrator himself. His work as *administrative leader* must be distinguished from other types of leadership. As the active and visible director of the council's life, he may naturally be led by his experience to assume the initiative for the creation of services that will extend far beyond the bounds of the council's work. He may indeed have to occupy much of his time in representative capacities, working in the community on behalf of the churches, and relating them to other bodies like welfare agencies or civic groups. As his experience accumulates, and his relationships in the community expand, certainly he will acquire a unique perspective that will lay on him a peculiar obligation toward the community. The ties he thus establishes and the duties he undertakes in his representative functions in the community may constitute a major section of what he does as the general executive of the council of churches. But these activities must be distinguished from his role as the administrator of the council.

His function in the council is to mobilize its resources—material, human, and spiritual—and relate them in a complete pattern so that they can be released for the accomplishment of the objectives to which the council is devoted. By his own relationship he draws these elements together, keeps them active, inspires them with purpose, and seeks to create the conditions for the success of their efforts. He does not need to know all about the specialized fields under his administration, nor does he have to exhibit all the skills needed by each department. It is his primary obligation to discern the many types of contributors that are needed, and to mobilize them, relate them to each other, and be able to judge when their contributions are effective.

The administrator may also have to take the role of the contributor for one or more parts of the whole program. This is especially likely in small councils, where the staff will consist only of the general executive himself. He will have

93

to serve not only as the general administrator, but like a director-actor in a drama, he may have to take the part of many of the contributors who would otherwise be the subjects of his administration. There will be some councils without any employed staff at all, who will nevertheless have to recognize the leadership of some one person—perhaps the president or someone else chosen on a voluntary basis—to serve as the executive leader. What is said here about the general administrator would apply, as far as time and capacity allow, to any voluntary leader.

The centrality here accorded the general executive requires that some consideration be given to the demands made on the person who undertakes this responsibility. In a sense he is a minister whose parish is the entire community. This offers a contrast in perspective from that under which the parish pastor labors. The parish minister comes inevitably to see the variety of his contacts and obligations in the perspective of his parochial ministry. The leader of a council of churches, on the other hand, must, like a businessman whose constituents are drawn from the entire community, see the community in its wholeness, and try to lead the council to minister to the needs of the entire community. This means that he himself will have to have a carefully worked out and conscious philosophy of the council he leads and of his relationship to it. He will have to acquire as rapidly as possible a complete understanding of the community and its needs, be willing to accept the large-scale responsibility involved, and to work with a daring initiative. He will have to achieve a patient urbanity based on a creative and sometimes revolutionary plan of action. As administrative leader he is at the same time related to the council as an organization, and to the whole group of churches that constitute it. As an executive his function is always to find and release the resources needed to accomplish the whole task. As community leader he will frequently have to withstand the temptation to build a personal program, much as a local pastor may do, around the skilled and professional activities that he himself could carry out; but to do this would mean dooming the council to an exceedingly restricted program. An executive can accomplish a large task only if he constantly devotes himself to the direction of the labor of others. He actually accomplishes through someone else everything he does. For this he needs an exceedingly well poised and patient outlook on his duties and his relationships.

The work of the executive has been thus—in a rather exaggerated fashion—described:

"As nearly everyone knows, an executive has practically nothing to do except to decide what is to be done; to tell somebody to do it; to listen to reasons why it should not be done, or why it should be done in a different way; to follow up to see if the thing has been done; to discover it has not; to inquire why; to listen to excuses from the person who should have done it; to follow up again to see if the thing has been done, only to discover that it has been done incorrectly; to point out how it should have been done; to conclude that as long as it has been done, it may as well be left where it is; to wonder if it is not time to get rid of a person who cannot do a thing right; to reflect that he probably has a wife and a large family, and that certainly any successor would be just as bad, and maybe worse; to consider how much simpler and better the thing would have been done if one had done it onself in the first place; to reflect sadly that one could have done it right in twenty minutes, and, as things turned out, one has to spend two days to find out why it has taken three weeks for somebody else to do it wrong."*

This bit of whimsey nevertheless highlights the essential nature of the work of the council executive. He is really most effective when he himself is withdrawing from the actual point of action.

To summarize, we might conceive of a council of churches as a vehicle in which a group of people are taking a trip. The vehicle is the organization. The executive may be thought of as the driver; his major concern is with the effectiveness of the machine. But to make the machine accomplish its purpose, the driver has to know the objectives of those taking the trip. He has to know not only where the car is going but how to get there. He will have a real concern about the relationships of the people in the car, for their congeniality and interest in the whole enterprise, and be able to use their contribution toward the achievement of the ultimate goal. The executive process, therefore, is the effective use of the means at hand toward the accomplishment of the purposes of the council itself.

---

* Quoted from *The Mission Tower Messenger,* Westwood Hills Congregational Church, Los Angeles.

Chapter 15

FINANCE
· ·

W. P. Buckwalter, Jr.

No one pattern of finance can be blueprinted to serve even the majority of our councils of churches across as diverse a country as the United States. Nor do we want a single pattern; principles and procedures should be adapted to fit the specific needs of different communities. From such adaptations and experiments better processes evolve that strengthen co-operative Christianity.

The experience of older councils is that the finances of our council cannot be placed in a separate pigeonhole apart from the other phases of our council's life and work. Nor can finance be considered a "business" aspect of our council, in contrast to its "spiritual" programs, activities, and services. To be effective and to enlist sufficient leaders of the right quality, finance must be as spiritual as any other phase of our council. Even to think of finance as merely business is to emasculate our approach to every source of income.

The income of our council is not an end in itself. It is one of many segments in a circle: program, activities, and services motivate both groups and individuals to carry on God's work by investing some of their God-given assets to create an additional or a better quality of council programs, activities, and services to our fellow men, women, and children. As to "which comes first, the hen or the egg," we cannot wait for either money or program to be present first, because they create each other.

Many councils do not have a financial policy or any financial principles; they have only procedures. Existing "from hand to mouth," they try to secure enough income to meet their immediate and pressing needs, often in the closing days of the fiscal year after most of the money has already been spent. This is the hardest kind of fund-raising and the least productive. Such councils, constantly unable to meet their responsibilities have a millstone around their necks, which in turn affects every decision they make about program, activities, and services. Members of these finance committees, as well as other officers and leaders of such councils, become discouraged and drop out. New leadership, especially chairmen of committees, become harder to find. In such an atmosphere new churches do not unite their strengths in the co-operative mission of Christianizing their community. Churches that participate in the marginal activities of the council do not become more active. Churches that have been active hesitate and falter; and the cumulative effect puts such councils on a treadmill—going through the motions but getting nowhere.

Many of the principles and much that is said in this chapter duplicates and overlaps what is being done by other sections of our council that has been mentioned in other chapters. And it should. What one member of a body does influences all the other members. Correlation among finance, publicity, public relations, and in fact all phases of the work of our council must be very close, because they are part and parcel of successful financing.

The following principles and procedures are not all-inclusive. They must be taken into consideration in the development of the financial policy of our council, especially if our present needs are to be met and if we are to finance the co-operative work of Christianizing our community to reach the 40 per cent of our population who are not connected with any religious group. These principles and procedures are certainly guideposts that must be considered, whether in this order or some other.

Representation

The financial policy of our council requires development by as widespread a representation of the entire constituency as possible. Each denomination; small, medium, and large congregations; the various geographic areas; laymen and laywomen; ministers; older leaders and younger executives—each group has contributions to make in developing our financial policy.

Those who have gone through the educational process of studying the problem, exploring various ways and means used elsewhere, and then determining the financial principles and procedures to fit the particular needs of our council, are much better equipped to secure the acceptance of our polyglot constituency. If a person or group objects or hesitates, but can talk with his representative who has been through the educational process, the understanding and response will be quicker and more productive because they both speak the same language, work with the same types of people, and have the same problems. Since laymen, laywomen, and ministers are the leaders involved in making the financial decisions in our council's constituent bodies, spokesmen for each group are required among those who have taken part in the educational process of developing the financial principles and procedures.

Many councils develop a financial policy or a yardstick of giving, and then wonder why only a few churches respond and put the procedure into practice. Usually it is because a few representatives of perhaps the larger constituents went through the educational process of seeing the entire situation, considering a variety of solutions, and then evolving a plan of action. The downtown churches, or the small denominations, or any other segment of our council, who have not gone through the educational process, thus do not have anyone who can interpret the adopted procedure to bring about their acceptance and the desired response.

Since several years are usually necessary to develop, communicate, and secure the general acceptance of financial principles and procedures, our council is wise to have a third of new members elected to the finance subcommittee each year. Those who are in their second and third years of service can interpret the policies so the same ground does not have to be covered each year, and the cumulative effect of the principles can grow with the years. The duties of these older members can include ex-officio membership on the other committees of the council, because the services of all committees and programs must be communicated as the finance members seek funds. Such assignments also help to train future chairmen and vice-chairmen for the various financial subcommittees.

Stewardship

The spring that spiritually activates our council's financial machinery is stewardship. Our space limits what should be said about stewardship; but three convictions interject themselves into our financial thinking, policy decisions, and procedures.

First, our council financial policy should be an extension of our denominational stewardship beliefs and practices.

Second, we need to remember that Jesus said, "For where your treasure is, there will your heart be also" (Matt. 6:21). Until the constituent bodies of our council accept their responsibility to finance their creation adequately, with its programs, activities, and services instigated by their official delegates, our council probably will plead in vain for the necessary leadership and responsiveness to become a creative, evangelizing force in service to our community.

Third, when their treasury obligations have been accepted and come to be practiced by our constituent members, the concomitant values in time and talents will demonstrate what the prophet Malachi meant in saying, "Bring the full tithes into the storehouse, that there may be food in my house; and thereby put me to the test, says the Lord of hosts, if I will not open the windows of heaven for you and pour down for you an overflowing blessing" (Mal. 3:10).

Care must be exercised, however, that our finance committee does not overemphasize the tithing of treasure alone; our council needs the whole man and the whole woman, with their full tithes of time, talent, and treasure. Our finance activities should produce their share of gifts of time and skills and abilities for co-operative Christian work, as well as money, from the stewards of God.

Service

Service is important in raising money, even as it is the lifeblood of our council as a whole. Jesus said to his disciples, "A servant is not greater than his master; nor is he who is sent greater than he who sent him. If you know these things, blessed are you if you do them" (John 13:16-17). Even so, our council is weak or strong in accordance with the fervor with which it forgets itself and serves the community (city, county, state, nation, world) in implementing our daily petition:

"Thy kingdom come,
Thy will be done,
On earth as it is in heaven" (Matt. 6:10)

Financial service is dual in its outreach: service to member churches, and the service to others that contributors wish carried out to bring the good news to each member of the community.

Though it is true that followers of Christ should not think of financial support to their council in terms of what they themselves are going to get out of their council, but rather of their responsibility to finance God's co-operative work through their council, it is also true that many churches are in the adolescent stage of spiritual development and consequently do think in such selfish terms. For this reason—but even more because our council has a Christian duty to aid its members to follow the teachings of Jesus—our council's financial policy must include service to help our constituents to strengthen and increase their own financial resources. Stewardship Institutes promoted by our council among the churches in each neighborhood reiterate the denominational emphasis. Both the denominational and the co-operative approaches strengthen each other, and help local parishes to develop their own stewardship program. The sharing of joint problems and successful techniques reduces the fear of new and untried procedures, and those congregations that are stronger or have developed better methods lead the nearby churches to more successful ways of fund-raising. Often a Stewardship Institute leads to a united church canvass, with the neighborhood churches co-operating in their use of the joint program and accumulated experience of the forty-seven denominational stewardship groups. If our council renders such a service, it helps its member churches to help themselves.

As our council members become stronger financially, they become more willing to take up their proportionate share of the financial responsibility for their council. This in turn permits them to do those things in the community, through their council, that all know should be done, but that they have not been able to do, because of inadequate finances in their council treasury. Perhaps we put the cart before the horse in asking for financial resources to carry on program activities before we render the service that demonstrates our council's ability to be a good steward. Contributors, whether groups or individuals, are usually ready to finance the organization that is accomplishing what the contributors want done.

Policy

A most important step in developing a financial policy is to take sufficient time—a two- or three-hour session is best—to write down the answers to four questions:

1. What are we doing now to finance our council?
   (a) What are its strong points?
   (b) What are its irritating aspects?
2. How do we want our council to be financed ten years from now?
3. Which one, two, or three steps should we concentrate on this year to
   (a) provide sufficient funds for our present work?
   (b) be developed further in the years to come so that we can have their cumulative effects?

99

4. What steps should we take next year, and in following years, to provide the means of expanding our Christian influence into every home and life in our community?

One session will probably not suffice to answer these questions; perhaps an evening for each will be necessary. The best time to begin is within a month of completing your money-raising effort. Most campaigns fail to reach their goal because we do not allow enough time for thinking through, planning, recruiting, and training the right leadership, and carrying out our policies and procedures.

Probably three to five years will be needed to develop a sound financial policy fitted to the particular needs of our council. This is why the policy should be written out and then modified after careful consideration and trial. Many councils swap leaders in the middle of a campaign without the manpower or the lines of communication to produce satisfactory results. Other councils change their financial procedure each year, and thus confuse their constituency and lose the cumulative values that come in the second, third, and fourth years.

The financial policy is a star to which we hitch our wagon. Unless we know where we are going, we are apt to arrive at our destination without the money necessary to carry on God's co-operative work in our community for the coming year. Another way of looking at it is to consider our council to be financially on the first floor of a house. Where we want to be ten years from now is on the second floor. Few of us can get from the first to the second floor in one step; but all of us find it fairly easy to take one, two, or three steps upward each year. We often reach our goal sooner than we expected because of the cumulative efforts, and because we know where we are going and how we are going to get there.

Sources

The sources of income that our council will decide to develop depend on what it is trying to do; why it was organized and by whom; what concept it has of its responsibility to God, to its constituent members, and to the parts of its community not yet reached by any religious influence; all of which will be reflected in our answer to the four questions listed under policy.

If we are a council of churches, the delegates officially elected by the governing body of each local congregation, parish, or church will constitute our council. Consequently its authority rests in the electing bodies. The activities, programs, and services that these official delegates decide to carry out co-operatively through our council will be merely an extension of each local church as a part of Jesus' command to "preach the gospel . . . to the whole creation" (Mark 15:16) which will cost something in time, talent, and treasure from each constituent. Therefore the constituent bodies of our council are one, if not the main, source of income that should be developed.*

Twenty sources of income that other councils of churches are using are listed

---

* *Financial Counseling #1, Financing Our Council of Churches*, 10c each.

100

in a tabulation made yearly since 1952.* The relative percentage of the total income—both by population groups and by the amount of income—is also given in this document, which should be consulted by each finance committee before it develops its financial plans. The five largest sources of income in each of the three categories, with the percentage of total income, are:

Councils with Paid Leadership
40 State Councils

Denominational budgets   24.4
Individuals   23.7
Program fees   10.5
Local church budgets   8.3
United church women   5.3

201 City and County Councils

Local church budgets   28.1
Individuals   27.1
Community chests   8.2
Offerings   6.8
Program fees   6.3

Councils with Volunteer Leadership
150 City and County Councils

Local church budgets   47.8
Offerings   26.6
Program fees   7.0
Local church organizations   5.6
Individuals   4.3

These figures give the sources of income from 391 councils reporting, of the 935 councils in 1953. Income from community chests is designated as income from social, health, and welfare activities, and not for religious programs and services.

In deciding which sources should be developed by our council, we have to keep in mind the discussion later in this chapter on primacy; but in the end each source is composed of individuals. Men and women in the pews of the churches are the ultimate source of all income from parish, denominational, and co-opera-tive work. As stewards of God they express their spiritual development by the way in which they use God's blessings to them to carry out his work as it is called for by the Holy Spirit. They not only give to our council through their church and their church organizations, but they go the second mile and con-tribute again as individuals of their time, talent, and treasure directly to our council.

These individuals should not be cut off from this second-mile giving by hav-

---

* *Financial Counseling #3, 1953 Income Tabulation and Other Financial Data,* 50c each.

101

ing their pastors, church finance committee, or governing board make it a condition of the church's corporate gift to our council that the individuals or the local church organizations are not to be solicited. Denominational leaders, as well as fund-raisers, know that these individuals, who have learned the spiritual satisfaction that comes from using their assets in response to the leading of the Holy Spirit, are the best workers and givers. Nor do such multiple givers reduce their contributions to their local church or denominational cause; the records show that they increase their giving to all causes.

Corporations and business firms composed of religious-minded individuals contribute to councils of churches among other philanthropic causes for a number of reasons. Religious teachings and precepts are the basic foundation of the American free enterprise system. Stockholders, employees, and customers of every firm are Jewish, Orthodox, Protestant, and Roman Catholic, and the council of churches is recognized as the Orthodox and Protestant co-operative agency in the community. Corporations are also interested in having strong religious agencies in the community, so they will be able to attract and keep, as executives and workers, the type of people they need for a successful business enterprise. The best way for our council to develop this source of income is to get a number of men and women who are already active in our council to secure contributions from their firms. Then our workers are in a strong position to ask other firms to give to our council, especially if they can say that those closest to it—its constituent members and church organizations—have already done their share.

Gifts from corporations are still few and small in most councils. Several years more of interpretation and education will be necessary before our council can expect to have a considerable percentage of its income from this source.

Primacy

It is generally accepted in our country that those who create and control the policies of an organization also have the responsibility to provide the finances necessary to carry out their plans and decisions. One of the authorities on philanthrophy* makes two generalizations as to the motivation of givers: those who are most active in the leadership, and those who directly benefit from the activities of an organization, are its best financial supporters. Fund-raisers have built successful business enterprises on the theory that those closest to the organization must be the first contributors, since their gifts are the pace-setting or yardstick gifts that result in successful money-raising efforts.

For our council of churches this means that our council family is the first to be approached for financial as well as other types of support and leadership. In our immediate council family we have both a group and individuals: the group is composed of the constituent members of the council; the individuals are the members of the finance committee, the officers and members of the executive committee, the trustees, the professional and office staff members—if our council

---

* F. Emerson Andrews, *Attitudes Toward Giving*, Russell Sage Foundation, 1954.

has paid leadership—and the members of all council divisions, departments, commissions, and committees.

From our council family the circle widens to both the local church organizations and the pastors, laymen and laywomen leaders, and all the members of the constituent churches. A few (92 of the 935) councils are beginning to develop a source of income from local church organizations.* Practically all of us readily accept the concept that individual church members become stewards of God within the financial orbit of their creation, their council of churches. Some of us will question an approach to the minister for a personal contribution to support ecumenical Christianity in his community. But if we don't, how can any minister persuasively and effectively ask the finance committee and/or the governing body of the church of which he is the spiritual leader to support financially their council of churches unless he himself has first done his part? Or can he preach the stewardship of God's bounty to the members of his congregation until he sets a personal example? This one procedure may be the key to the adequate financing of our council. It is not the amount, individually or collectively, that the minister gives. The important thing is that he himself has first done what he is asking others to do.

Another group of individuals that some councils consider a source of income is made up of those who are nominal church members on the roll but who are not active in attendance or in the financing of their church. The writer has yet to discover a council that has more than a handful of such contributors; their giving is negligible in the total income. The stimuli that motivate givers come from consistent attendance and work within their own church; consequently those who are most active in their own churches are the best workers and contributors to their church, their denominations, and their council of churches.†

The last group to be approached is the community as a whole: community chest or united fund for social, health, and welfare projects; foundations and trusts for grants to carry on specific programs within the scope of their interest; and the corporations and business firms in our community. This latter group should not be approached until after the immediate council family and the local church organizations and individuals have done their part—unless you are seeking only small token gifts. First things must come first, for successful council financing.

Proportion

In connection with the different sources of income to be developed, our finance committee will determine what percentage of the total income should be sought from each source. But proportion is also important in connection with the constituent members of our council.

When we talk to the finance committee, or the governing body, of a constituent member of our council, almost always we are asked: "What is our share?" Our council finance and/or executive committee will have to develop some

---

* *Financial Counseling #3, 1953 Income Tabulation and Other Financial Data*, 50c each.
† F. Emerson Andrews, *op. cit.*

yardstick by which each constituent member can distinguish and accept its financial responsibility in carrying out God's co-operative mission to evangelize and convert our community. Five methods* are currently in use by the councils of churches, and all of them work because the constituent members have agreed to make them work. Briefly they are:

1. *The Realistic Approach*—based on what was given last year and what is hoped can be secured this year. This leads to arguments as to whether this or that church is carrying its fair share of the financial load.

2. *The Sliding Scale or Fixed Percentage*—churches in each designated expenditure bracket contribute the set percentage. Both bracket and percentage are arbitrarily selected, thus "loading" the yardstick against the large or the small, the rich or the poor, the strong or the weak congregation.

3. *The Per Capita Fee*—ranges from two cents to a dollar per individual member of each constituting body. "Member" is an arbitrary term with a different meaning and standard in various denominations: active, resident, adult, communicant, constituent, etc. There are councils where this discussion is a major item on the agenda of most meetings. Councils, as well as denominational bodies, are changing to a percentage-of-expenditure basis.

4. *The Proportionate Percentage Plan*—the total expenditure (omitting new building, major renovations, mortgage payments) of all the constituent members is divided into our council budget (the cost of what the officially elected delegates of the constituent members have agreed should be the co-operative programs, activities, and services of the congregations and parishes through their council each year) to secure a percentage figure. This figure is then multiplied by the total expenditure of each constituent member church to determine its proportionate share in dollars and cents. New councils are starting with and old councils are switching to this yardstick probably because it is the simplest, most easily explained, most impartial, and most objective yardstick yet developed.

5. *The Combination Plan*—plans 3 and 4 are combined to create two factors for this yardstick. It retains all the disadvantages of the one and adds no strength to the other.

All five of these yardsticks have variations to suit the traditions, precedents, mores, and divisions of particular councils. Some city councils feel that a second or modified yardstick should be used for churches in suburban or distant points in the county that receive only partial benefits from the programs, activities, and services of their council. Other councils feel that 2 per cent from a constituent member with $5,000 expenditures ($100) may be a greater burden than 2 per cent from one with a $50,000 expenditure ($1,000).

At the other end of the scale more and more churches are contributing more than 100 per cent of their proportionate share, just as a very small percentage of individuals (around 10 per cent) in every congregation contribute the largest percentage (over 75 per cent) of its income. Of 606 churches in 11 councils

---

* *Financial Counseling #1, Financing Our Council of Churches*, 10c each.

reporting in 1952,* 26 per cent were contributing 100 per cent of the asking from their council, and another 6.6 per cent were giving more than 100 per cent. These are the churches that not only preach stewardship but practice it as a corporate body in accepting their fair share of the financial support of their council of churches—or even more than their share.

Broad Base

Two aspects of the broad base of the pyramid of giving need to be constantly in the mind of our finance committee. We need a broad base in the number of the sources of income for our council—sources described above.

The second aspect is often carried by councils of churches to an expensive extreme: securing too large a number of small individual contributors. The *1953 Income Tabulation* shows that 77.7 per cent of the individual contributors to state councils, 74.7 per cent of those to city and county councils with paid leadership, and 93 per cent of those to volunteer councils, are giving $9 or less per year. This survey did not ask for the amount contributed in each category by individual givers, but the 1952 survey† of 33 councils with 29,782 individuals giving a total of $332,788, shows that 69 per cent of the contributors, giving less than $9 each per year, gave 21 per cent of the total amount. Such a pyramid is little more than a base; it has very little above the foundation to supply funds to carry out God's co-operative work in our community.

College alumni funds have shown that a yearly gift of $5 results in little more than goodwill. It costs that much to secure, acknowledge, record on class, school, and alumni records, not to mention the professional, office, and volunteer's time and ability. In a few cases, a cost accounting of securing and servicing these smaller gifts to our councils would reveal that money is actually being diverted from program to secure additional small gifts that, in turn, drain more money from program! To be sure, these small gifts have some value in publicity and public relations, but cannot these values be earned more cheaply, effectively, and widely by straight publicity and public relations techniques?

The professional fund-raiser would also ask: "Is a gift in such small amount really a contribution to carry out God's work, or is its token given so as not to hurt the feelings of the asking friend, to salve the conscience of the giver, or to stop these written appeals for another year?" A sermon by Peter Marshall, "A Tip or a Tithe,"‡ emphasizes that many Christians give God only the loose change in their pockets.

Sell Our Product, Not Our Cost

Because the goal of our council's financial effort is usually published as an amount of money, we forget that this goal is only an intermediate stopping point and not our final destination. We think and talk about the $5,000,

---

* *Financial Counseling #2, 1952 Income Tabulation and Other Financial Data,* 40c each.
† *Financial Counseling #2, 1952 Income Tabulation and Other Financial Data,* 40c each.
‡ Julius King (ed.), *Successful Fund-Raising Sermons,* New York, Funk & Wagnalls, 1953.

$10,000, $30,000, or $100,000 budget until the amount appears to be our objective. This means that we are "selling" the cost of our council.

We forget that a budget or a money goal is only a means to an end, and in itself has very little power to inspire a proportionate or generous contribution. It is not the pledge or the money that counts; the important element is what the gift of money will produce in bringing religious influences into the lives of five or ten individuals. The spiritual dividend produced by a gift to our council of churches is found in the changed lives of those who are reached and affected by our council's programs, activities, and services.

Generalities and vague statements that our council is reaching this or that group will not sell our product. We need to use not only factual statements but also exact figures. Rounded or guess-estimate figures create in the mind of the hearer or reader a feeling that this is a casual, dreamy project that the speaker or writer does not consider important enough to dignify with actuality. The more we can interpret the figures, tersely, the greater impact they will have. For example, which does the better selling of our product: "We had a large and successful leadership training school this year"; or "One hundred ninety-four leaders attended the seven evening sessions of three hours each in our leadership training school. Their increased knowledge and skills affect an average of ten boys and girls, each of the 39 weeks in the church school classes of 15 churches in 6 denominations. Each of these children carried their religious training into nearly 2,000 homes to the other 6,000 members of their families, as well as to their associates at play and school."

In selling the spiritual product of our council, we must continually and constantly supply our public with facts about all the programs, activities, and services rendered by Orthodox and Protestant individuals and churches through their councils of churches. Only then will they take pride in their accomplishments and provide the time, talent, and treasure to produce more spiritual dividends.

Look at the advertisements in our magazines that mention the same product week after week and month after month. Count the number of full-page advertisements that do not even mention a price, or that print the price in small type down in one corner. These business firms are selling their product, not its cost. Much more, we, in financing our council, need to sell its spiritual products. These, not the amount of money to be raised, motivate individuals and local churches to contribute their fair, proportionate share of the cost.

Manpower and Womanpower

The minister cannot be expected to carry the full ecumenical responsibility of his church, especially not in the financial field. Laymen and laywomen are more effective than ministers, because they are volunteers, and because they can talk the same language on the same level with other laymen and laywomen. Then again, most churches have only one minister, but hundreds of lay people. How many churches are a spiritual force unless they enlist many laymen and laywomen for each minister? Too many councils are now limping along with a handful of people trying to do the total financial task. The handful becomes so discouraged by the magnitude of its task that it merely goes through the motions.

Laymen and laywomen have skills and abilities that they use in earning their daily living. Yet how many of them are asked to use these skills, these abilities, and this know-how, in God's work, either in the parish or in our council? Many are asked to be deacons or teachers, for which they have no training, and they respond eagerly though conscious of their own lack. Many from the sales and related fields can bring skills and know-how, which they are using daily, to the financial work of our council.

To begin an adequate financial program will require in most councils several subcommittees with eight to twelve people on each. Each subcommittee will have a specific job of developing one source of income throughout the calendar year. The chairmen of the subcommittees could constitute the policy-making executive committee on finances, so that each group of workers will know what the other subcommittees are doing without multiplying the number of meetings for all members. Some councils may object that such a number would be nearly as many persons as we now have in all the work of the council. But most of us know that we are not going to accomplish what we know we can do in God's name until we have more adequate manpower and womanpower.

Frequently the men and women who conceive a project or extension of the program services of our council will produce the necessary finances for the undertaking, either from their own resources or among their friends as individuals and as members of the groups to which they belong. An experimental or pilot project may be thus financed for two or three years, until it demonstrates its place in the regular budget of our council. Many councils have in this way convinced the doubting Thomases, and have expanded their council's outreach and service.

Communication

As this chapter has shown, effective communication is a weak link in our council's financial program. The men and women in the pews, who are the only financial source for all parish, denominational, and co-operative Christian work, do not know what they and their church are now accomplishing through their council. How, then, can we expect additional money from them?

Our council, to secure adequate finances for co-operatively Christianizing our community, must develop ways and means of reaching at least ten men and ten women in each parish with sufficient information to convince them of their churches' corporate financial responsibility. Even then we are assuming that these twenty, with their minister, will be strong enough to convince their congregation of hundreds or thousands of members to contribute enough to enable their council to operate. Eventually we must certainly reach a larger number of the men and women in the pews if we are to provide sufficient funds for making our community more Christlike.

Councils are discovering that one financial leaflet a year is not enough—not even when 20,000 copies are distributed in the pews of churches in a city of 250,000 people. Additional leaflets every year, as well as the use of the other media of publicity and public relations, are necessary to rouse the people in our churches.

Factual data, the use of actual figures to show the scope and ramifications of what our churches are doing through their council, are always more effective than the rounded estimates used in many of our present leaflets. Too often our written material is so vague and wordy, as we try to cram every activity into each financial leaflet or issue of our council's house organ, that it ends up without producing any effect on the reader.

Every delegate to and worker in our council should report, at each monthly meeting of the governing board of the church that appoints him, what his council is accomplishing. As each delegate becomes a two-way channel of communication between his church and his council, the governing board of each will accumulate facts on which to base their policy decisions.

Although communication is not usually the responsibility of the financial leaders, they will have to stimulate good communicative practices if the atmosphere is to be helpful when finances are mentioned.

Time

All of us have learned in football, tennis, and other sports, that timing is one of the fundamentals. Without it we cannot be successful. Timing is also an important basic element in money-raising. In both sports and finances we do not achieve this necessary timing until we have had preparation and practice and a plan of procedure.

Too often our council and its constituent members try to conduct a financial effort in a few weeks so the balance of the year can be devoted to our real job of program and service. We forget that neither can exist separately. Since they have to exist and grow on each other, they both need to be carried on through all the months of the year. Developing and practicing successful fund-raising procedures are a responsibility the year round of any devoted group of laymen and laywomen.

Time must be taken to evaluate what we have done, and to plan for what we are to do, step by step, month by month. Merely to recruit the right persons to do the right job at the right time, we have to secure their commitment several months in advance, or some other worthy cause will have them tied up when we need their stewardship of time and talents—skills, abilities, and personal influence.

Tasks must be divided so that many hands make light work of the job, and this also requires time for planning and co-ordination. Many money-raising efforts get only within striking distance of their goal because not enough time has been spent in planning, organizing, recruiting, and training our leadership. In such cases we reach only 70 per cent to 90 per cent of our goal instead of going over the top.

Fund-raisers are often asked, "When is the best time to raise money?" The answer—which is not as facetious as it sounds—is, "When you have to have money!" Only then are most of us willing to do a good job of preparation, planning, recruiting of leadership, and to use in large enough amounts our personal time, talents, and treasure.

Mission

Each church and each council of churches, as a corporate body, has a mission that must be fulfilled if it is to be a spiritual force. Perhaps it is not within the province of the financial leaders to define the mission of our council. But it certainly is the duty of the financial leaders to see that funds are available for the present undertakings of our council, and to see that we also have more for unforseen opportunities.

Does not our council have a responsibility to provide at least one new activity or service each year as a cutting edge of Christianity, to expand and reach religiously a new group of people, or another section of our community, or to raise the standard of an accepted service by providing the financial resources to do a better job than we have been doing? Unless our council, as well as our local church, grows spiritually from year to year, it will wither and fade away. If our council does develop spiritually, it will be more sensitive to the guidance of the Holy Spirit, and will see more and more what needs to be done to make our prayer come true:

> "Thy kingdom come,
> Thy will be done,
> On earth as it is in heaven" (Matt. 6:10)

These spiritual insights will in turn require more time, talent, and treasure from the stewards of God's bounty.

One need for which we should be prepared may be the expenditure of a considerable sum of over six or nine months in preparation for a teaching or preaching mission, which, when it is held, will pay for itself. Another contingency for which a finance committee with a sense of its mission will provide, is the paying of the salaries and bills of our council during the three or four months of each year when we have little if any income. No business can stay open long without operating capital. As stewards of God, we laymen and laywomen have an obligation to see to it that the best business practices and procedures are used in our churches and our councils of churches.

Such a revolving or operating fund should not exceed the year's budget requirements of our council; if it does, it probably indicates too small a staff, unmet program needs and services, and/or a deadening of our spiritual development as a council, in that we are not aware of God's work that our council should be doing.

Chapter 16

PUBLIC RELATIONS

· ·

Donald C. Bolles

A Modern Concept

Public relations are basically as old as the human race; but public relations, as a technique, is a twentieth century innovation. All human beings, unless they live in complete isolation, have public relations. These relations are their contacts with other people, who touch their lives directly or indirectly. The relations may be good or bad, as they are conditioned by the interplay of personality, opinion, or conduct.

The modern concept of public relations envisages a well conceived strategy to develop and nurture favorable public opinion. It involves the measurement of the temper, tempo, and taste of the public, and a concerted effort to communicate information through the most effective channels to help develop favorable attitudes and stimulate action.

This concept springs from the dependence of institutions for their success and perpetuation on the belief of society that they are in the public interest. It was born in a democratic world that insists on the right to information on which to base its judgment, and its experience that error is induced by ignorance.

The church has had public relations for more than nineteen centuries. In fact, no institution except government can be said to have had a longer record in dealing with people. Because it has been concerned with the souls of men, the church's public relations are unique, and cannot be compared with those of any other institution.

Through all its history the church has served one Master, and but one purpose—Christianity. It has sought from all men and women a favorable decision for the way of life of the New Testament. The church, in its ceaseless effort to evangelize the world, has faced many public relations problems, born of man's selfishness and the isolation of many from the knowledge of the Gospel.

In the early centuries the church was compelled to rely for communication to a large degree on the voice of the disciples reaching the ears of those willing to listen to the story of Jesus Christ. There was no other channel of communication, and many lived out their lives without knowing the way to salvation.

110

Everyone May Hear

In these modern times the problem of communication has been solved by man's inventive genius. Today there are few places in the world where those who serve the church cannot communicate the good news of the Gospel to those who can see, hear, and read. Today the church faces a different problem in communication; life is a thousand times more complex than in the early days of Christianity. In the eternal conflict between God and mammon for the fealty of man a thousand secular interests vie with the Gospel for his attention. And on the rock of Christian faith the church as an institution has developed world-wide activity that can be sustained only by the support of its members.

This means that *the church must be visible to the whole community*, like the steeples that once dominated the horizon for all to see. And *the church's voice must be so powerful that it can rise above the din of daily life*.

The church does not stand out on the horizon, nor does its voice rise above the din, when there is no co-ordination of the efforts of the churches to make the people conscious of the relevance of the Christian Gospel to the problems of their everyday lives. Their fragmentary picture of the church presented by each parish alone does not make the church sufficiently visible to the community, nor does it make an impact on the consciousness of people with any degree of effectiveness compared to that of a joint effort. The community is usually interested in what affects the whole community; only occasionally in what happens in one church.

The Present Community Picture

Only our common concerns, the work we do together or on parallel lines, our efforts to stir the moral conscience presented vividly in terms of the interests of all people, through church and public channels of communication, can make them conscious of the indispensable part the churches play in the life of the community.

This approach may secure for the church the *understanding, acceptance,* and *support* it requires as an institution; it can also assist evangelistic efforts by arousing the interest of unbelievers and others who profess belief in God but shun worship in his house. We do not pretend that a program of interpretation through channels of communication will add converts. It may arouse interest, but the task of winning souls to Christ rests where it always has— on ministers and dedicated lay people.

The religious picture that is of interest to the whole community can be presented effectively. It requires the churches to consolidate many pictures of religious activity to form a mosaic. This picture must bring all activity into focus to portray a true picture of the church and its mission.

The formula for thus successfully interpreting the church involves the use of various channels of communication, and telling the story to the public that each channel reaches, in terms of its *knowledge* and *interest*. The daily press, for instance, is used to reach all the people in the community, when

111

the story is of general interest, but not as a vehicle to communicate information of interest solely to members of one congregation. Such information is communicated through bulletins, calendars, and other channels the parish maintains.

Judged by Two Standards

The church should not only use all available channels of communication, but should also adapt its story for each channel in terms of the interests of the audience it reaches. The story will be judged by two standards of interest: First, the church's; and second, the channel of communication—such as the press, broadcasting, and magazines. This means that those who serve the church must know the standards by which all channels, church and public, gauge the interest of their audiences. All public channels are aware, in varying degrees, that the revival of interest in religion is at a peak for this generation.

The churches have, in the council of churches, both the organization and the spirit necessary to present their story in terms of community interest. Our churches constitute a council to counteract the weakness of division, and to lend strength to their ministry by doing together what can be done better together than separately.

Planning and Public Relations

The council, dependent for its perpetuation and growth—as well as its influence in community life—on favorable public opinion, needs effective interpretation as much as it needs a purpose for life. This suggests that the council should give public relations a place with policy and program at the planning table, and insure the fullest contribution by public relations to the council's whole life, by making available to it whatever resources are required to function effectively.

The existence of the council provides the churches with a vehicle not only to interpret the council's program, but also to develop the fullest co-ordination in achieving the strongest possible impact on the community.

Nine Public Relations Principles

To assure effective public relations, a council of churches should consider nine principles:

1. The public relations task is to gain and nurture understanding, acceptance, and support for its purposes, programs, and objectives, from the people of the community, and particularly from those it serves and those who serve it.

2. The goal of all public relations efforts is to gain favorable public opinion for all the good purposes of the council and what it represents in the community. Specifically, it should seek to insure adequate leadership and financial support, to extend the influence of its program, and to insure support when the churches choose to speak as one on moral and social issues.

There are times when, in obedience to the mandates of the Gospel, reaction in the community may be antagonistic. In such situations it is the task of public relations to assist in interpreting the churches' position and in achieving understanding of it.

3. Publicity is a handmaiden of public relations, as the story it tells helps create favorable opinion.

4. Every aspect of the council's life that affects public opinion should be considered part of the public relations task.

5. The public relations function, to make it serve the council's total interests, must be harnessed to policies, program, and procedures.

6. Public relations must be a concern of the governing body and its administrative director. The task must enlist the help of all who are responsible for directing the council.

7. The program of interpretation, devised to develop and nurture favorable opinion, should utilize every avenue of communication and every method of presentation that can be effective.

8. The interpretation must be adapted to the interests and comprehension of the public reached by each channel used—newspaper, radio or TV station, magazine, church paper, or meeting.

9. The council's public relations is a primary consideration that requires the same degree of competence, imagination, and industry that other phases of its work demand from the dedicated Christians who serve it.

With these principles in mind, the council should proceed to plan its public relations program and organization. No blueprint can be devised, of course, that will be satisfactory to everybody. Guided by its own needs and resources, each council must agree on the plan that will best serve its total interests.

Organizing a Program

The following seven steps may be used as a guide in formulating a plan for organization and a program:

1. Create a small planning committee that will represent the council's leadership, and include laymen in the community who are conversant with public relations procedures and techniques.

2. Authorize the committee to make a full investigation of the council's needs in the light of its objectives, and devise a comprehensive plan of organization, and procedures and program to integrate public relations functions into the council's total operations.

3. Make the plan an integral part of the council's structure and activity, and finance its needs for staff and general funds out of the council's regular budget.

4. Establish the administrative responsibility for public relations with due regard for priorities, the part others must take, and the technical skills and physical limitations of the staff.

113

5. Determine what machinery is required to insure the full integration of the public relations function, giving consideration to any of the following:

    a. A central department of public relations, operated by those who are familiar with policy, program, and public relations, to advise the council and to provide such guidance and assistance as the program of the council may need.

    b. An advisory committee of laymen engaged in various phases of public relations, which may be called on by the public relations director for advice.

    c. Staff conferences to permit the frequent review of public relations aspects of the program, and thereby give the public relations director an opportunity to make suggestions, provide counsel, and keep in touch with all activity.

6. Establish as soon as possible the position of public relations director as a part of the council's executive staff; this director to report frequently to the board of directors, and to be responsible administratively to the executive secretary, who shall have general oversight of the director's work.

7. Employ a public relations director who by training and experience is the best qualified the council can find and afford to pay.*

These steps will enable the council to carry on a public relations program. The suggested procedures will help put public relations thinking into every phase of the council's life. Success depends a great deal on administration.

Qualifications for Public Relations

To find the best qualified person for full-time operation as public relations director the following minimum requirements should be kept in mind:†

1. An active church member with a deep-seated desire to serve the churches, and a sound understanding of the nature and role of the church.

2. Mature and personable, with a knowledge of what interests people, and an ability to produce stories acceptable to the press and other media.

3. Experience in some aspects of public relations or publicity—preferably one trained in newspaper work.

4. A teamworker, qualified by temperament or experience to accept the conditions under which the council must work.

The public relations task involves a wide variety of activities. The council should look to the public relations director to provide leadership in this aspect of the council's life, and to undertake himself the services that will be most productive. To interpret the council through publicity in all media

---

* A council of churches that is not able at first to employ a full-time director of public relations has the following alternatives: to assign responsibility to a qualified member of the staff; to employ a qualified part-time director; to secure a qualified volunteer, preferably someone engaged in the public relations field.

† These same qualifications apply equally to a volunteer or part-time director.

should be his primary consideration, but his potential service will be seriously reduced if he does not advise with those who are responsible for policy and program.

Effective public relations depend on *quality;* and attempting too much may prove a disservice to the council. Sound planning, research, and analysis that reflect the judgment of all who are able to help the public relations director in any phase of his activity, are the kinds of painstaking effort that is the hallmark of quality.

The public relations aspects of a council or churches are extensive—more so than generally recognized. They provide a virtually limitless opportunity for service by those who have a working knowledge of public relations as well as the techniques of publicity. Recognizing that the competence of the director and time both impose limitations on what may be accomplished, a council should consider the whole gamut of public relations tasks and formulate a program of action as a goal. It may indicate priorities as a further guide to those who administer the program, as it makes a selection from the nineteen public relations tasks listed here.

1. Counseling with the board of directors and with the executive secretary about the interpretation and other public relations aspects of over-all policies and plans.

2. Counseling with the members of the staff and committees about the public relations aspects of literature, statements, letters, and other material, and the special audiences to which they are directed.

3. Helping to plan the observance of special weeks and days, such as Christian Education Week, Reformation Day, World Day of Prayer, Labor Day Sunday, Race Relations Sunday, and others.

4. Planning the public relations aspects of meetings, conferences, and seminars held by the council or with its co-operation.

5. Helping to plan programs or events to bring the council and its program to the attention of community leaders in government, business, labor, agriculture, and the professions.

6. Arranging seminars for clerical and lay leaders of local churches, to promote better understanding of the philosophy and techniques of public relations.

7. Arranging "get acquainted" sessions of church leaders with those who direct newspapers and broadcasting, so as to develop better understanding of the church and the functions of mass media.

8. Disseminating all news concerning the council to the daily, weekly, and neighborhood press, and to radio and TV stations, and personally cultivating those who handle religious news in these media.

9. Providing a steady flow of information concerning all phases of the council's life that are of special concern to the constituent churches, their clergy and members, through a regularly published council bulletin, and for use also in parish papers and calendars.

115

10. Arrange special radio and television programs to publicize the council's program and leadership, and provide advice about the public relations aspects of programs of worship and Christian education.

11. Make available to the *Religious News Service, Religious Newsweekly* (published by the National Council of Churches), *The Christian Century,* the *National Council Outlook,* and occasionally to denominational and secular magazines, stories and articles of more than local interest, about religious activities and personalities.

12. Handle public relations at all major meetings of the council, and offer similar services to synodical, diocesan, or district conferences of the constituent communions that are held in the community, under an arrangement mutually agreeable.

13. Publicize those council leaders who participate in community affairs and events in which the council may or may not be a sponsor.

14. Develop visual exhibits that portray the council's program, for use at church conferences and in local churches.

15. Maintain a speakers' bureau. Recruit for it both clergymen and laymen to fill all requests and solicited invitations; and provide them with a wide variety of informational and anecdotal material.

16. Develop informational literature—pamphlets, reprints, and the like— in a persistent campaign to cultivate a variety of audiences.

17. Serve as a clearinghouse for general information about the council, and answer or refer inquiries that come by mail, telephone, or personal calls.

18. Maintain a public relations library of information—biographies, photographs, minutes, reports, mimeographed and printed material—about the council and its leaders, and its member constituent churches and their leaders.

19. Direct the public relations aspects of the council's annual financial campaign, as well as keeping it in mind in year-round efforts, so as to create a climate that will sure a favorable response to the council's financial need.

The Goal—Favorable Opinion

Favorable public opinion is the goal of the public relations program that has been outlined. The importance of such opinion cannot be overemphasized; on it depends much of the vitality one council contributes to church life, the influence of its Christian message on society, the moral and financial support the council receives; in fact, to a degree the very existence of the council. Public relations, given adequate tools to work with, and the full support of leadership, can certainly increase the breadth and depth of the council's influence in the community as an effective instrument of Christianity.

Chapter 17

RESOURCES AVAILABLE FROM THE
NATIONAL COUNCIL OF CHURCHES
. . . .

J. Quinter Miller

The resources of the National Council of Churches that are now available to other councils are of two types—program and staff. The first consists of program plans, ideas, and source materials that cover a wide range of inter-denominational ministry and service. Some of these program resources have been specifically prepared to help the churches as they work together in states and local communities; others are designed for nationwide promotion and development. They are available as aids in strengthening Christian co-operation wherever church council leaders desire to use them.

The Office for Councils of Churches, and the General Departments of United Church Men and United Church Women, are also specially equipped to share the successful experiences of one council with another. GROWING TOGETHER is itself such a medium of experience sharing. The program and field operations of the National Council as a whole seek to make available to state and local councils as much of the National Council program resources as these may wish to use.

The second resource consists of the staff of the National Council. This staff is a kind of experience library, which like a university draws from a very wide range of experience in Christian co-operation. To the limits of time and work load, each one of these National Council colleagues is a resource person to help the churches advance their co-operative work. This is some-times accomplished by direct service to the member communions. At other times the co-operative ministry needed requires an interdenominational ef-fort, and consequently the state and local council workers find that national staff colleagues are teammates in a common task.

Using the organizational structure set forth in Chapter 6 as a pattern for listing the most likely areas of program assistance we list the following:

Division of Christian Education

Gerald E. Knoff, executive secretary, 257 Fourth Avenue, New York.

Harry H. Kalas, associate executive secretary, 79 East Adams Street, Chicago, Illinois.

A. L. Roberts, general director, Commission on General Christian Education and associate executive secretary of the Division, 79 East Adams Street, Chicago, Illinois. (The areas of work covered by this commission include: Children's Work, Young People's Work, Adult Work, Leadership Education, Church School Administration, Curriculum Department, Weekday Religious Education, Vacation Church Schools, Audio-Visual and Radio Education, Christian Family Life, Religion and Public Education.)

Philip C. Landers, director, Committee on the Use and Understanding of the Bible, 257 Fourth Avenue, New York.

Hubert C. Noble, general director, Commission on Christian Higher Education and associate executive secretary of the Division, 257 Fourth Avenue, New York. (The areas of work covered by this Commission include: The Interseminary Committee, Student Volunteers. The United Student Christian Council, Christian Vocation, *The Christian Scholar,* Campus Christian Life.)

J. Allan Ranck, general director, Joint Commission on Missionary Education and associate executive secretary of the Division, 257 Fourth Avenue, New York. (The areas of work covered by this Commission include: Missionary Education materials for Children, Youth, and Adults, Audio-Visual Education, and Summer Conferences on Missionary Education.)

Division of Christian Life and Work

C. Arild Olsen, executive secretary, 297 Fourth Avenue, New York. (The areas of work covered by this division include: International Affairs, The Church and Economic Life, Racial and Cultural Relations, Pastoral Services, Religious Liberty, Social Welfare, Worship and the Arts, Evangelism, Stewardship and Benevolence.)

Division of Foreign Missions

Luther A. Gotwald, executive secretary, 156 Fifth Avenue, New York. (The areas of work covered by this division include: 1. Co-operative Missionary Service in Africa, Southern Asia, Japan, Latin America, the Near East, the Philippines, Southeast Asia, and Okinawa; 2. Co-operative functional services through the Associated Missions Medical Office; Christian Medical Council for Overseas Work; Audio-Visual Education and Mass Communication; Rural Missions; Treasurers; World Literacy and Christian Literature; Co-operation with Churches in Europe; Interchange of Christian Leadership; Missionary Personnel; Public Relations; Relief; Research; The Christian Approach to Communism; Technical Co-operation; American Communities Overseas.)

Division of Home Missions

I. George Nace and Edith E. Lowry, executive secretaries, 257 Fourth Avenue, New York. (The areas of work covered by this division include: The Urban Church; The Town and Country Church; Share Croppers; Indian

118

Work; Migrant Work and particular specialized mission needs in Alaska; The Christian Approach to the Jews; Defense Communities; Home Missions Institutions; Missionary Personnel; the West Indies; Youth and Student Work.)

General Department of United Church Men

Edwin W. Parsons, general director, 257 Fourth Avenue, New York. (The areas of work covered by this department include: Churchmen's Week, Laymen's Sunday, meetings in key cities, assistance with state and local organization, support of Christian colleges, religion in industry, Christian missions, and national convention for Christian men.)

General Department of United Church Women

Mrs. W. Murdoch MacLeod, general director, 175 Fifth Avenue, New York. (The areas of work covered by this department include: Christian World Missions; Christian Social Relations; Christian World Relations; Leadership Training; Public Relations, Radio, TV, Films, Audio-Visual, Press; and Special Observances—World Day of Prayer, May Fellowship Day, World Community Day.)

Broadcasting and Film Commission

S. Franklin Mack, executive director, 220 Fifth Avenue, New York.

Central Department of Church World Service

R. Norris Wilson, executive director, 215 Fourth Avenue, New York.

Office for Councils of Churches

John B. Ketcham, executive director, 297 Fourth Avenue, New York, and 79 East Adams Street, Chicago, Illinois.

Office of Public Relations

Donald C. Bolles, executive director, 297 Fourth Avenue, New York.

Office of Publication and Distribution

Norman E. Tompkins, executive director, 120 East 23rd Street, New York.

General Administration

The responsibility for administering the total work of the National Council is vested in the office of a General Secretary. The General Secretariat consists of the following:

Roy G. Ross, general secretary, 297 Fourth Avenue, New York.
Roswell P. Barnes, associate general secretary, 297 Fourth Avenue, New York.

J. Quinter Miller, assistant general secretary for Field Operations, 297 Fourth Avenue, New York.

Leila W. Anderson, assistant general secretary for Program, 297 Fourth Avenue, New York.

Wilbur C. Parry, assistant general secretary (at large), 297 Fourth Avenue, New York.

Earl F. Adams, assistant general secretary (Washington Office), 122 Maryland Avenue, Washington, D. C.

J. E. Luton, assistant general secretary for Administration, 297 Fourth Avenue, New York.

Richard Smith, assistant general secretary for Finance, 297 Fourth Avenue, New York.

A complete list of all staff members of the National Council of Churches by departments may be found in the current *Yearbook of American Churches* or in the *Biennial Report 1954,* National Council of Churches.

BIBLIOGRAPHY
. . . .
Joseph M. Woods, Jr.   J. Quinter Miller

ANDREWS, F. EMERSON, *Attitudes Toward Giving*, New York, Russell Sage Foundation, 1954.

ATHEARN, WALTER SCOTT, *Religious Education and American Democracy*, Boston, Pilgrim Press, 1917.

BARNARD, CHESTER I., *The Functions of the Executive*, Cambridge, Mass., Harvard University Press, 1942.

———, *Organization and Management*, Cambridge, Mass., Harvard University Press, 1948.

BILHEIMER, ROBERT S., *The Quest for Christian Unity*, New York, Association Press, 1942.

BOWER, WILLIAM CLAYTON; HAYWARD, PERCY R., *Protestantism Faces Its Educational Task Together*, Appleton, Wis., C. C. Nelson Publishing Company, 1949.

BROWN, WILLIAM ADAMS, *Toward a United Church*, New York, Charles Scribner's Sons, 1946.

BRUNNER, EDMUND DESCHWEINITZ; HALLENBECK, WILBUR C., *American Society: Urban and Rural Patterns*, New York, Harper and Brothers, 1955.

CASSADY, MAYNARD L., "The Significance of the Community for the Religious Situation," *Crozer Quarterly*, Vol. XXVI, No. 1, Jan. 1949.

CAVERT, SAMUEL McCREA, *Christian Unity in America*, New York, Charles Scribner's Sons, 1936.

CRAIG, CLARENCE T., *The One Church*, New York and Nashville, Abingdon-Cokesbury Press, 1951.

DAWBER, MARK A., *Rebuilding Rural America*, New York, Friendship Press, 1937.

DOUGLASS, HARLAN PAUL, *Protestant Co-operation in American Cities*, New York, Institute of Social and Religious Research, 1930.

DOUGLASS, TRUMAN B., *Mission to America*, New York, Friendship Press, 1951.

DUN, ANGUS, *Prospecting for a United Church*, New York, Harper and Brothers, 1948.

HARMS, JOHN W., "The Development of Protestant Co-operation in Baltimore, Maryland, from 1919 to 1949," unpublished thesis (M.A.), University of Chicago, 1952.

HARTSHORNE, HUGH; MILLER, J. QUINTER, *Community Organization in Religious Education*, New Haven, Yale University Press, 1932.

HUTCHISON, JOHN A., *We Are Not Divided*, New York, Round Table Press, 1941.

JOHNS, RAY, *Executive Responsibility*, New York, Association Press, 1954.

KING, JULIUS, ed., *Successful Fund-Raising Sermons*, New York, Funk and Wagnalls, 1953.

121

KNAPP, FORREST L., *Handbook for Councils of Churches in Massachusetts*, Massachusetts, Councils of Churches, Boston, 1955.

LATOURETTE, KENNETH SCOTT, *A History of the Expansion of Christianity*, New York, Harper and Brothers, 1945.

LOTZ, PHILLIP HENRY, *Studies in Religious Education*, Nashville, Cokesbury Press, 1931.

MACFARLAND, CHARLES S., *Christian Unity, in Practice and Prophecy*, New York, Macmillan, 1933.

MACKAY, JOHN A., *God's Order*, New York, Macmillan, 1953.

MILLER, KENNETH H., *Man and God in the City*, New York, Friendship Press, 1954.

MORRISON, CHARLES CLAYTON, *The Unfinished Reformation*, New York, Harper and Brothers, 1953.

MORSE, HERMANN N., *Toward a Christian America*, Missionary Education Movement, New York, 1935.

NEWBIGIN, LESSLIE, *The Household of God*, New York, Friendship Press, 1954.

————, *The Reunion of the Church*, New York, Harper and Brothers, 1948.

NICHOLS, JAMES HASTINGS, *Evanston, an Interpretation*, New York, Harper and Brothers, 1954.

NIEBUHR, H. RICHARD, *The Kingdom of God in America*, Chicago and New York, Willett, Clark and Co., 1937.

————, *Social Sources of Denominationalism*, New York, Henry Holt and Co., 1929.

PIERREL, GREN O., *The Executive Role in Y.M.C.A. Administration*, New York, Association Press, 1951.

ROUSE, RUTH, NEILL; STEPHEN CHARLES, eds., *A History of the Ecumenical Movement, 1917-48*, Philadelphia, Westminster Press, 1954.

RUML, BEARDSLEY; GEIGER, THEODORE, eds., *The Manual of Corporate Giving*, Washington, D. C., National Planning Association, 1952.

SEIFERT, HARVEY, *The Church in Community Action*, New York and Nashville, Abingdon-Cokesbury Press, 1952.

SKOGLUND, JOHN E., *They Reach for Life*, New York, Friendship Press, 1955.

SORENSON, ROY, *The Art of Board Membership*, New York, Association Press, 1950.

SWEARINGEN, TILFORD, *The Community and Christian Education*, Bethany Press, St. Louis, 1950.

TEAD, ORDWAY, *The Art of Administration*, New York, McGraw-Hill, 1951.

————, *Democratic Administration*, New York, Association Press, 1945.

TRECKER, HARLEIGH B.; GLICK, FRANK Z.; KIDNEIGH, JOHN C., *Education for Social Work Administration*, New York, American Association for Social Workers, 1952.

VAN DUSEN, HENRY PITNEY, *World Christianity, Yesterday, Today, and Tomorrow*, New York, Abingdon-Cokesbury Press, 1947.

VIETH, H. PAUL, *The Church and Christian Education*, St. Louis, Bethany Press, 1947.

Wedel, Theodore O., *The Coming Great Church*, New York, Macmillan, 1945.
Wyckoff, D. Campbell, *The Task of Christian Education*, Philadelphia, Westminster Press, 1955.

PERIODICALS

The Church Woman, National Council of the Churches of Christ in the U.S.A., New York.

Ecumenical Review, World Council of Churches, Geneva, Switzerland.

International Journal of Religious Education, National Council of the Churches of Christ in the U.S.A., Chicago.

National Council Outlook, National Council of the Churches of Christ in the U.S.A., New York.

Biennial Report 1954, National Council of the Churches of Christ in the U.S.A., New York.

Christian Faith in Action, New York, National Council of the Churches of Christ in the U.S.A., 1951.

Handbook (National Aspects of Co-operative Christianity in the United States), National Council of the Churches of Christ in the U.S.A., New York, 1952-1953.

Yearbook of American Churches, National Council of the Churches of Christ in the U.S.A., New York.

Note. Bibliographical materials of a special functional or departmental nature will be furnished on request. Because of their broad scope, they have not been included in this bibliography.